Relentless

By

Kevin O'Hagan

Published by **New Breed publishing**

Printed by

New Breed Publishing
Po box 511
Dagenham
Essex RM9 5DN

www.newbreedbooks.co.uk

Printed in Feb 2004 (1st edition)

Cover design by **Thomas O'Hagan**

A CIP catalogue record for this book is available from the British Library

Printed and bound in Great Britain.

ISBN 1-904432-05-0

Please note: The theoretical information and physical techniques outlined in this book are for self-protection and Self-defence purposes only. The author and the publishers cannot accept any responsibility for any proceedings or prosecutions brought or instituted against any person or body as a result of the misuse of any theoretical information or physical techniques described in this book or any loss, injury or damage caused thereby.

RELENTLESS

My endless pursuit of the warrior way

Dedication

For my Mum for fighting back against another serious illness. Keep strong and keep the faith.

Acknowledgements

To each and every person who has taught, inspired and guided me in my Martial Arts journey. There are too many to name but I thank you all. Special thanks to my training partner, fellow instructor and true friend Rob Cannon for all your tireless work and dedication.

Love and thanks as always to Tina for typing up the manuscript and the kids for teaching me computer skills!

About the Author

This is Kevin's fifth book to date, all published by New Breed, the leading light in practical Combat and Martial Arts books. Kevin is a well-known and respected Martial Artist in the field of reality Combat, self-protection and the Mixed Martial Arts/Cross Training scene. He runs regular clubs in the Bristol area and teaches on the UK seminar circuit. As well as a professional Martial Arts instructor of nearly 30 years, he is a qualified fitness\sports coach. He writes regularly for 'Fighters' magazine and has produced ten unique videos of his Combat system.

Other Books by Kevin O'Hagan

I thought you'd be bigger, *a small persons guide to fighting back.*
In your face – *Close Quarter Combat.*
Grappling with Reality – *Survival on the floor.*
Bad to the Bone – *Exploring the many facets of Aggression and Violent Behaviour.*

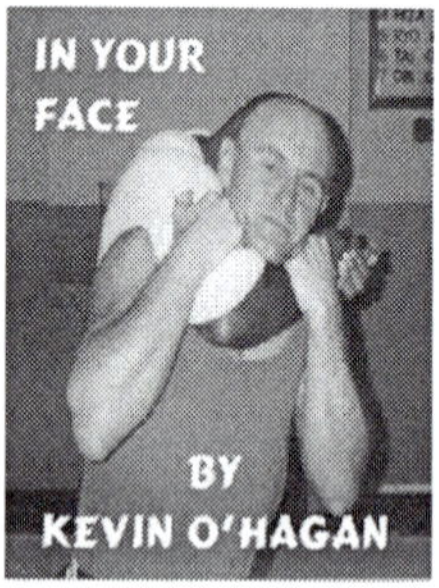

Preface

When I initially developed the idea for this book, I sat down and thought long and hard about whether anyone would want to read about my life in the Martial Arts. After all there were more experienced, talented and successful individuals in the Martial Arts world that haven't yet put pen to paper, so why did I feel I had something different to offer?

With that thought in mind I decided to put the project on the back burner and go on with other activities in my life. I had too many doubts about the whole idea, so I tried to forget about it.

Fifteen months later I re-visited the project and this time viewed it in a more positive light.

Firstly I realised I had devoted a quarter of a century and then some, to the Martial Arts. I can honestly state that in all that time there have been very few occasions when I haven't been training, trying to improve my abilities and absorb more and more information. Until recently at forty years of age I competed at professional level in mixed Martial Arts Competition. There are few sportsmen or athletes who stay that long in their chosen disciplines. In this country when a sportsman reaches thirty years of age he is deemed "over the hill". If they continue beyond this they are thought of as somebody really special.

I also noted how the Martial Arts had shaped my life and took me from a young, green and slightly insecure fourteen year old boy, along an exciting, challenging and many varied journey to where I am now. Along the way I have met some interesting characters. The good, the bad, and the MAD! I have made many true friends and been inspired by people of genuine class.

I've experienced a multitude of combat systems, traditional, modern and electic and gathered vast quantities of knowledge and know how. I have also sweated blood and tears for the cause and trained beyond what I thought a human being was capable of enduring.

As that young boy I never dreamt I could achieve the things I have done. On the big scale of things they may not seem important to those who have tasted greater and bigger success but for me from my humble beginnings I have moved a few "mountains".

My success cannot be measured in riches and monetary gain but from inner satisfaction of having reached some of my long-term goals in life which have given me much happiness, belief, confidence and strength. I have fought and conquered many of my internal battles and this in turn has given me a better life.

This book will track my time in the Martial Arts from beginning right up to present day. I will tell you my story straight, no fabrication, no exaggeration and no outlandish claims. I will tell it how it was, no punches pulled, the good and the bad. Hopefully it will entertain, inform and amuse as well as give great in-sight into the exciting and sometimes crazy world that is Martial Arts.

Introduction

The date is June 19th 2001 and it is my fortieth birthday. My wife Tina has organised a surprise party for me. Well a sort of surprise, I did know about it because she had to get names and addresses of friends past and present, but everything else was a surprise.

The party is a great success, you never know with these kinds of things. I am not a great party person and did have reservations especially about Liam Gallagher and Jordan showing up, but no worries were necessary! During the course of the evening I met many people who have made up my Martial Arts classes over the years. Some I haven't seen for 10 years or more but they came. They all had a tale to tell about their training days with me and would recount some anecdote about a particular aspect. They remembered details and facts I had long forgotten. It was amazing to note that although a lot of these guys were no longer part of my classes they still had great enthusiasm and interest in what I was doing. I realised that I had made a big impression upon their lives. Maybe it was all the brutal beastings I gave them that stayed in their minds, or it just might have been my sweet nature! Later when one of my most senior instructors Rob made a speech, it hammered home how much respect and feeling people had for me in that room. They had come from all over to be there and apart from my close family, I had somewhere along the line taught everybody else Martial Arts and they hadn't forgotten. I was greatly humbled and moved.

The month of June had been a good one for me; leading up to this party I had received a phone call from Sensei Dave Turton Chief instructor of the Self Defence Federation and Goshinwai Combat. Dave is a long time friend, an old instructor of mine and a man I greatly respect. The call was to inform me I had been promoted to 6th Dan Master grade is Combat Ju Jutsu by a panel of senior instructors. It was a great surprise and a fantastic early present. Days after I received a certificate from the British Combat Association, co-run by Peter Consterdine and Geoff Thompson telling me I was now a senior Self Protection instructor in the BCA, a great honour.

Also earlier on that month I had fought in the Combat Sport Vale Tudo National Championships with ML Sports. This was two weeks shy of my birthday and although I lost my fight to the young up and coming fighter Richard Stopgate, I was proud to still have had good fitness and technique to compete at this high level.

Things had really come together that month, it was a memorable time. I was a proud man that night and when the party was over and I sat and reflected in the quiet, I realised I had achieved much in my life, particularly in the Martial Arts and many people knew me because of this fact. Plus I had the respect of my peers, which is a hard thing to achieve, and one that is important to me. I had a loving and strong family behind me and I realised just how far I had come in the 28 years I had devoted to life to the Martial Arts. The journey wasn't by any means over but I did feel I had finally reached a peak. A peak where I could sit, look out at the views and be satisfied that I had got there. What's beyond this peak I don't know; only time will tell but first let's look back on how it all began? I close my eyes; settle back in this armchair with my feet up and a cold 'Bud ' at hand. In the stillness and silence and let my mind rewind. Rewind back through the years, right back to the start of the journey.

I will take you back to an era of space hoppers, Cresta soft drinks, flares and kipper ties. When Liverpool ruled the football world and Slade ruled the pop charts. A time of endless summers and holidays by the sea. A space in time when I had long hair and girls referred to me as being cute! Yes the good old 70's, my beginnings in Martial Arts. Then we will cruise the 80's, 90's and into the new millennium with my training and experiences across the decades. It's been a long voyage. Please don't abandon ship until we later dock.

I hope you enjoy reading this book as much as I enjoyed writing it. Let the journey begin, seconds out round one!

Kevin O'Hagan

Jan 2002

Chapter 1

'Early seeds planted'

I had a great interest in sport when I was a youngster. I loved to watch it and to play it, although I wasn't born with the natural skills of an athlete.

I was particularly interested in football and avidly followed it with a great passion. In the 70's I knew all the players from each first division team and many of the other leagues. I collected all the magazines, football cards, old programmes; I was quite a fanatic around the age of 10 or 11 years old. My favourite heroes of that time were George Best, Bobby Moore, Gordon Banks, Pat Jennings and later players like Kevin Keegan and Bryan Robson.

If I didn't have any mates to kick a ball around with I would play by myself in the back garden. Most evenings after tea I would be out there, homework conveniently forgotten about, lost in a fantasy world playing at Wembley, Old Trafford or Anfield

Over a period of years I wore the grass completely away and demolished my dad's 'beansticks' or 'cabbage patch'. I just loved to play wherever I could.

I remember on Sunday afternoons nagging my Dad to bring me up to the local park to kick a ball around with me. Looking back now my old man must have been knackered but he rarely let me down. He worked hard six days a week on the buildings and Sunday lunchtime he enjoyed a few pints down his local. Coming back and going up the park to run around for a few hours was probably the last thing on his mind, but he was always there for me.

Although I was quite small I was developing into a pretty good goalkeeper and enjoyed diving around all over the place. At school in the playground I was forever wearing holes in my clothes because I would dive at anything, no fear of the concrete.

I played for my school on a handful of occasions in goal and done all right. Later at 14 years old I played many times for the local school youth club in eleven and five a-side games. I still play now and again for my local Sports Centre in five-a-side tournaments; you guessed it, in goal. Still throwing myself all over the place and not a mat in sight! The old reflexes are still pretty sharp and I put that down to the Martial Arts.

Tracking back again to around twelve years old I also developed an interest in wrestling and boxing. I used to watch the wrestling on ITV's Saturday afternoon 'World of Sport'. This was British wrestling and although the bouts were 'worked' it had a gritty reality to it unlike the American stuff of today. Great wrestlers like, Marty Jones, Mark 'Rollerball' Rocco, Fit Finlay and Skull Murphy, were some of the top boys from that era and they really were tough men that could do the business for real if need be.

If rain stopped the Sunday afternoon kick around at the park, wrestling was next on the agenda! The living room floor was the ring and away Dad and me would go. I used to try all the moves I had seen on the television on my Dad and he would let me get away with so many and then suddenly pin me down. God, I worked up a sweat, everything with me was 100% full on. I always ended up red faced and soaked in perspiration, I remember those times vividly. My Mum used to be in the kitchen, (the place where all mums seem to live) washing up the Sunday lunch dishes and shouting out. "What are you two doing, you'll wear a hole in that carpet, stop it!" My Mum was very house proud (still is) and it used to wind her up but having said that she still let us do it!

I feel that at this stage I must mention my parents, Joe and Mary. Both were born and breed in Northern Ireland. My Dad lived later in Scotland for a time before coming to England and then brought my Mum over. They settled here in Bristol and my sister (Brenda) then later myself were born. They were always hard working, active and down to earth people. They both could be gentle or hard when needed and I suppose this is where my Irish fighting blood comes from and my steely determination to succeed in whatever I do. Our background is working class. Although we lived simply and times could be tough my childhood was generally a happy one.

They are both lives's fighters and continue to be so. For those of you who have read my last book 'BAD TO THE BONE' you will know I mentioned my Mum some years ago suffered a massive stroke, but has made a spirited recovery. Although not fully able she has been a shining example of fighting spirit, grit and determination. She inspires me to keep fighting and working at things if all is not going my way. (Whilst writing this book she has survived two more strokes which this time nearly claimed her life.)

Both my parents instilled in me at en early age the difference between right and wrong. Also that God helps those that help themselves. In other words don't sit moaning about what you could have done, get out there and do it!

My Dad worked hard all his life in the building trade. Mum tirelessly worked in the NHS. Both grafted hard for what they achieved in life. They have always been there for me with help and advice and I would like this chance to thank them both in print.

OK, back to the wrestling. At this time I also started watching some of the big boxing matches on television. Muhammad Ali was the main man in those early 70's, although my old man would tell me stories of Jack Dempsey, Joe Louis, Rocky Marciano and the fearsome Sonny Liston

When I was young I hated Ali and longed for him to be beat. I suppose at twelve or thirteen years old you wondered who this loud-mouthed, cocky and brash boxer was and I could remember being over the moon when the excellent Ken Norton beat Ali and also broke his jaw. Later on in life I realised just how good Ali had been and what an influence he had had on the boxing world.

Around this time of twelve I was bought a pair of boxing gloves and one of those punch balls on a stand, I loved it and whacked away at it daily. Although it used to whack me back just as much! Then come Sunday afternoon the front room would suddenly transform into Madison Square Gardens! I would fire away at Dad working up a lather, but usually it would end up in a wrestling match with me still firing punches on the floor. Come to think of it I think that was the birth of mixed Martial Arts and cross training although I didn't really have a clue what I was doing at the time!

These early memories show that I must have had a sub-conscious liking for fighting systems but football was always my first love. Although I had a passion for all sports I was hindered in developing in any of them and really missed my chance to excel. I will explain to you why.

I was born with my right leg slightly shorter than my left. This has caused me to walk with a slight limp all of my life.

When I was very young I hardly used the leg and dragged it along rather than throw it out to walk correctly. I constantly wanted to be carried or wheeled around in a pushchair (slightly embarrassing when you're 16 years old.....Only kidding!). Because of this I suffered muscle wastage to the leg and that has stayed with me to present day even after intense exercise to build it up.

There was a point in my young life where my Dad decided to lay the law down and try to correct my walking. He used to take me out for long and I mean long walks. He would constantly remind me to step out and use the right leg. He was having to be cruel to be kind, although at the time I didn't always realise the fact.

On occasions I would be angry, frustrated or cry. Its tough being constantly reminded to walk correctly whenever you stepped out of your front door. But with that steely determination I was developing I preserved with it all.

I also had to visit a specialist that manipulated my foot, ankle and rest of my leg in some weird and wonderful positions and gave me a series of exercises to be performed every day.

The ritual would be to do these exercises before I went to bed. I hated them and again there was much frustration, rebellion and tears. But once more I stuck at them.

Being reminded at home of your slight disability was tough enough but it didn't compare to the ridicule and piss taking I received at school. Kids can be very cruel and heartless and I experienced my share of this, especially at sport time. It got me into many fights, just out of pure frustration.

This began to drive me more inward on myself and to become ever more self-conscious about my problem. I became one of those kids at the back of a line to be picked for football, rugby etc, when I desperately yearned inside to be at the front. But all my self-confidence had been knocked for six. Looking back if I had been mentally stronger I could have done well in any sport as I proved later on in my life but then I was young, between eleven and fifteen it was a tough time, as there seemed to be a piss-taker at every corner I turned. Through all this part of me was determine to fight back and over come the disability.

I did find some respite by getting a chance to play in goal. As I mentioned quite earlier I had no fear of diving around, so I done quite well and was picked to be goalkeeper on many occasions. Amazing how one bit of talent can make people forget about your other shortcomings? The hours up the park with my dad had certainly paid off. But inwardly I felt slightly cheated when some of my mates were picked constantly for the school football, rugby, cricket or athletic teams. I felt I could have been there but for different circumstances.

I grew to live with my problems. I found balancing on the right leg hopeless, kicking a ball useless and things like climbing extremely difficult, I was ever conscious of these facts. To cap it all off I also had three bad injuries to the right ankle during my school days, which further weakened the leg and caused more problems. I have fractured my ankle, torn the ligaments, broke toes and sprained it countless times. On one of these occasions I jumped off a high wall whilst being chased by a gang of lads. I landed badly and struggled to regain my feet.

As the gang got closer I waited for the inevitable kick`in. But I was spared, as my two mates that were with me at the time came back for me and dragged me to safety. I had badly damaged my ankle. These weren't to be my last injuries either. Just recently I cracked the bone trying to escape a foot lock a very painful experience.

I was never what you could call a target for bullying but I did experience it on more than one occasion. At school for all my problems I was a bit of a joker and enjoyed a laugh. I certainly could have achieved a lot more in my schooling but I was too easily led into other things. I was never a troublemaker, more of a joker.

My reports always read," Could try harder", " Easily distracted," " Could do better", on them regularly. I liked English and Art, which funnily enough helped me considerably later on and I trained myself to make reading become a habit which I am so glad I did because reading can open up a treasure-trove of information. Over the years I have re-educated myself by reading and I am proud of that fact. I also never dreamt I could end up writing books and magazine articles.

Apart from the subjects mentioned I didn't really have much interest in school I just lived for the day and never really looked further than that. I hated homework and preferred to be in the back garden recreating anther cup final or punching my punch ball. I was quite smart when I put my mind to it but only if the subject interested me!

At 14 years old coming rapidly towards the end of my school career I didn't really have an idea what to do and just drifted along quite merrily. I was concerned I was small for my age and at 14 you become aware of your body (in more ways than one) and I decided I wanted to build it up more. I inwardly believed a few muscles would get any bullies or piss-takers off my back.

Up to that point I had experienced a few scraps and had performed in-differently. Looking back I lacked self-belief and now in hindsight realise some of the school tough guys weren't tough at all, they just had the mouth and the swagger so they got away with it (as have all live bullies).

I wanted to be tougher and stronger and I decided to do something about it. I was determined to succeed. At this time a mate of mine Robert Shepherd told me he was going to join a local gym in Bristol called the "Empire Club". This gym was one of the first and original in Bristol. It was a typical spit and sawdust gym. It was home for many hardcore body builders, weight and power lifters and it also had a boxing gym where a young Chris Sanigar did his training. Chris is now a famous boxing promoter in Bristol.

Weight lifter Precious Mackenzie was also a big name around this time in the mid to late70s. I was certainly keen to join and I told him I would try and get the money together to pay the membership fees. During this period in my life I suddenly came across somebody who would set about changing me for the rest of my life. I didn't realise the impact he would have on me and the influence but he did big time. This was the start of my Martial Arts journey, 1975. The man's name who started me on the road? The one and only, Bruce Lee.

"From little acorns mighty oaks grow"

Chapter 2

'Kung Fu Fighting'

I was in the changing rooms before a PE session, when I noticed a group of lads huddled around a magazine. Hold up I thought it must be another one of those 'girlie magazines' doing the rounds again. As I drew closer I heard gasps of amazement and voices exclaiming,' Look at that body' and 'Wow I never realised you could do that'. Getting a little excited I thought this is definitely one of those girlie magazines! But no, as I peeped over one lad's shoulder I saw something very different to what I expected. I saw this small, incredibly fit looking oriental man performing amazing kicks and strange looking postures. 'Who's that?' I asked.' Its Bruce Lee the kung-fu master' came the reply.

I can't recall having heard his name mentioned before this time and this was after he had unfortunately and tragically passed away. Surely I should recall his funeral on the news or pictures in the paper? But I couldn't. I only got to really know about him after he had died.

So here I was suddenly transfixed looking at this magazine. Incidentally it was called 'Kung-fu monthly', the one that used to open out into a poster of Bruce. I'm sure all you 70's Martial Arts Veterans will remember it?

I wanted to read it fully but the lad who owned it had already promised it to another 3 guys first. So I had to wait my turn. My turn came the following Friday, which was good because I got to bring it home for the weekend. I read every inch of it, absolutely amazed that this little man had such speed, power and ability. Before this I just presumed you had to be a big well-muscled guy to look after yourself, as portrayed in all the films and TV shows but here was something different. It gave me hope, it gave me purpose. I knew then and there I had to practice Kung Fu and wanted to be the next Bruce Lee (yes I was young and naïve) but that wouldn't dampen my enthusiasm.

Up to this point in time, which was 1975, I had heard very little about Martial Arts. Judo I had seen snatches of it on the television and in some films little bursts of Karate (mostly badly demonstrated). But after discovering Kung Fu, Martial Arts seemed to be popping up everywhere. This was the 70's Kung Fu boom.

The TV series 'Kung Fu' starring David Carradine arrived on TV! More magazines and books began to appear in the shops. (Remember the Bruce Tegner series of books?) The record 'Kung Fu fighting shot to the number 1 spot in the charts and everybody who ran the local Chinese takeaway was a secret Kung Fu master. It was crazy but exciting for me.

I remember Bruce Lee's 'Enter the dragon' playing at a local cinema and I just had to see it. The film was a certificate 18 and I of course was only 14! So on went the platform shoes and big overcoat and away I went and amazingly got in! The film was on a double bill with 'Freebie and the Bean' starring James Caan who incidentally is a fanatical Martial Artist.

I sat through that film, the commercials and the interval without moving. I didn't risk going to the toilet or buying a drink incase somebody suddenly discovered I wasn't old enough and threw me out.

When eventually 'Enter the Dragon' came on I sat there totally transfixed. To see my hero on big screen was an exciting moment. Bruce Lee had a screen presence and charisma that I personally don't think has ever been replaced. Even now when I watch one of his movies, his presence and class just shines through. When I exited the cinema I was in a daze and I walked home in a trance. The film had been everything and more to me and I was completely sold on Martial Arts. I wanted there and then to take on a gang of bullies with a series of chops, kicks and blood curdling screams. I wanted to rip off my shirt and expose the lethal claw marks on my person. Shit, I wanted to join the Shaolin Temple!

I was absolutely determined to start training and when I saw an advert in my local newspaper for a Kung Fu class starting I had to go. I persuaded my mum to lend me the money for my first session and away I went at 14 years of age into the unknown.

Unfortunately the first experience of Kung Fu came to an abrupt halt, when after the first session the instructor told me if I wanted to come back next week I would have to bring a £25.00 joining fee. This was a lot of money at this time and my parents couldn't afford it. Plus they were apprehensive, as the national newspapers had run a few articles about bogus kung Fu instructors taking joining fees and then disappearing into the night! So I never went back to that class. But I did remember and practice the moves I had been shown.

About six weeks later another advert appeared in the local paper. Once again a new Kung Fu class was being opened in a church hall in the centre of Bristol by the bus and coach station.

Once more I asked my parents if I could go and they said yes. So off I went again. This time the experience was altogether different. The club was looking for new members but it had already been established for a while. When I entered there was a small group of us waiting, we could see the class through the open door and it looked great. It was mostly guys all in black gi's with various coloured sashes around their waists practising different moves.

The system was a Southern Shaolin one, called Pak Mei (White tiger). The instructor was Sifu George Taylor from Birmingham. He had classes all over the country and travelled down to Bristol on a Friday for this particular class.

This time there was a modest membership fee for which you got a black T-shirt and black gi bottoms and a membership card. Come back next week and you can start. I couldn't wait.

Next week I was there and ready to go. A few of my schoolmates had also said they would start but at the last minute the let me down. My best mate Robert had decided to join the Empire Club after all and he went on over the years to win umpteen weight lifting championships at school boy and senior level. Even lifting for Wales in the commonwealth games. He practically lived at the Empire and the owner Dennis Welch treated him like another son.

It all got a bit much for Rob later, too much too soon I think and he gave it all up for a time. I feel he had the potential to be an Olympic champion if he had stuck at it. He was very good and we had some tough times at the Empire together, which I will speak about later. So basically I was on my own and the youngest guy in class but although part of me was scared the over riding need to do this out weighed the fear. I was in and going to see it out whatever it took.

These days the training was basic and hard. The class ran from 6.00pm to 9.00pm. The first hour was pure conditioning. Hundreds of knuckle press ups on the wooden floor, sit-ups, leg raises and deep knee bend squats. These would be repeated over and over again in cycles.

Being a young lad my muscles used to be screaming with fatigue. I can remember being at the back of the large class one week.

My position was right by a table where Sifu Taylor's wife collected the weekly fees. Under the table lay her two dogs. I don't recall what breed they were but they were big and ugly! I swear every time I stopped doing a push up or a sit-up, they would growl directly at me, as if to say get on with it!

I tell you there is no better motivation to keep going when your head or backside is only inches away from a growling dog's jaw.

Other training would involve hard and continuous forearm blocking to condition the forearms. Sometimes I left the classes and my arms were purple. I would have a job to hold my pen or knife and fork for days after. Also you would be kicked around the legs and punched and kicked in the body. All to build up toughness and conditioning. This was not too bad unless you ended up with a partner who had no control! Sparring was rough and brutal and I used to initially dread it but I suppose after numerous beatings your ego and fears diminish. For a young lad fighting grow men it was tough experience but I kept coming back.

The class was filled with many weird and wonderful characters. All wanted to be the next Bruce. Some nights there would be 60 or 70 people crammed into the hall sweating and shouting going through punches, kicks and strikes up and down in lines.

Another one of Sifu's little ploys was to start the class off with a 'little run'. Now bear in mind the venue was really close to the main Bristol City centre and nightlife, and that most people on a Friday evening were in town for a drink and a night out. Next minute they would see a group of 'black pyjama' clad men running along with Kung Fu badges emblazing on their gis. They didn't know whether to be frightened or laugh. Personally I kept tight in the middle of the group to save ridicule or getting the shit beat out of me!

Circuits were another love of George Taylor's. We would do an hour of this, running from station to station in the hall. The stations were all different. Punch bag at one, kick shields another, free-weights, callenstics, partner drills etc.etc

At one end of the hall was a stage with steps leading up one side and down the other. One trick was to run up those stairs with a partner on your back or shoulders and come down the other side. At this time I had a job to get somebody on my back, let alone climb the stairs! Plus my bad leg was just too weak. A few times I tried and fell miserably. It became my nightmare everytime circuits were mentioned and I dreaded it.

All those feelings of insecurity came flooding back and I hated it. But there were some good guys who helped and encouraged me. It was good of them to spend time with a youngster.

One guy whose name I can't recall became my training partner. He only had one arm and had a special light, metal one made so he could do his moves and his push ups.

I really admired his resolve and spirit to train and if he accidentally clocked you with his 'bionic arm' you certainly would know about it! I have a senior student with me now called Darren Sim who also has one arm, but you just wouldn't realise it as he adapts so well to technique and will also box and wrestle competently. He came to me already as a high ranked Aikidoist and is now a black belt in Ju Jutsu.

Sifu Taylor used to keep dreaming up different drills for us to test ourselves. Another one of his tortures was to pile up a small stack of metal backed chairs and get us to practice high kicks over the top of them. As we became more proficient he would add another chair. This all had to be done in bare feet. Many a toe was stubbed, foot smashed or shin cut doing this demanding drill (I can personally testify to all the above injuries). Also he would get you to try flying kicks over the chair backs. This was another of my nightmares, often ending in a tangle of metal, arms and legs. For all this I enjoyed the classes! They certainly sparked my interest in fitness, built my confidence and gave me a chance to practice my beloved Kung Fu.

Sifu Taylor was a good instructor and he had a few good senior lads as well. Two bright and up and coming stars were the Davis twins, Andy and Chris, who have gone on to very high achievements within the world of Taekwondo and kick boxing. I bump into Andy now and again these days and occasionally we will have a laugh about those early training sessions.

Another episode that sticks out in my mind vividly was when we would all run through punches, kicks and stance work as a class. Sifu would halt you in stance and come around and check your posture. He was brutal and unrelenting in kicking or sweeping out anyone's legs if they weren't in the right position. I must admit I didn't like or agree with this but this was how it was done back then.

One night we were all brought to a halt and Sifu began walking around the lines. Starting at the back and working this way up. That particular evening I was at the front of the class, (at least I was away from those bloody dogs!). I would hear bodies hitting the wooden floor like skittles. You daren't look back, you just had to wait and sweat. I could hear him getting closer. I heard a grunt and a slam behind me as another one bit the dust! Next to me were a young couple that had started that evening, husband and wife I think. They were stood understandably in the wrong posture, but then it was their first night. I had more important things on my mind like avoiding a trip to the floor.

Suddenly Sifu appeared by my side and then proceeded to circle me. Could he sense the slight tremor in my body? I hope to God the legs would not shake. I tell you, you wouldn't have been able to slip a cigarette paper between the cheeks of my ass! I gritted my teeth waiting for the impact, but no, he had moved on. I breathed a sigh of relief. Then he was by the young lady who had started that night and without a word he just swept her leg out and she crashed to the floor in a heap. Her 'husband' looked down at her and then at Sifu Taylor and for a moment I thought he was going to have a go at him but I think something in Sifu's eyes made the man change his mind.

These were tough times in Martial Arts classes. The fighting was hard, no pads or protection. Black eyes, cut lips and bruised ribs were common place.

The class stayed open for around two years until unbelievably the numbers dwindled from around seventy members a dozen. It just wasn't profitable for Sifu Taylor to travel all the way form the Midlands anymore. He did give us plenty of notice but it was still a disappointment when he left. I had reached orange sash which was the third grade and I felt I was really beginning to get the hang of things. I was 15 years old now and school was coming to a close. I really still had no direction in what I wanted to do, those Friday night training sessions were all I cared about.

I can recall a really funny incident around this time. Every week I would get a bus back home after training and I would usually end up with the same driver. He was a really nice coloured guy, who always spoke to me and had a bit of a laugh. One night he asked me where I went every week with my training bag. I told him Kung Fu classes. He replied he didn't rate all that oriental stuff, but I told him it was great. He wanted to prove his point and like in the classic line in 'Enter the Dragon' he said 'show me some'. So here we are facing each other in the aisle of the bus. Being the first stop the bus was empty except for a couple of 'old dears'. He came at me like a boxer and I lashed out a series of roundhouse and hook kicks, the last one catching him lightly on the face. 'Whoa, that's enough man, you proved your point', he says and we laugh and shake hands. I don't know what the old ladies thought of out 'impromptu' sparring session and now I laugh and can't believe we done this on a bus!

When Sifu left about eight of us decided to club together and hire the training hall and just carry on practising together until something else showed up.

So you start pooling ideas. The Davis brothers had been doing some Judo so by digging out a few old mats we started to combine a few throws and a bit of groundwork. It was good fun and kept us training.

I was beginning to get stronger in the last six months. A few of us at school with the help of Rob had persuaded the PE teacher to let us go to the 'Empire' club in our games period. At this time we were too young to body build so we had to learn weight lifting instead, this didn't work out how I thought it would and I ran into more problems.

"Slow progress is better than no progress at all"

Chapter 3

'Another Direction'

As mentioned in the last chapter when I went to the 'Empire' I really wanted to build my body up and increase my strength to aid my Martial Arts training. Dennis Welch the owner told me I had to be sixteen years old to enter the body building gym but learning to weight-lift would be fine. At the time I thought as long as I was working out with weights it would be all right. So each PE period I went to train.

Dennis wanted me to compete in competition but it was not what I wanted to do. He had seen Rob begin to do well and thought I might be interested as well. Instead of speaking up and telling him what I thought, I just got roped along.

The weight rooms were separate to the main gyms. I remember going down an alleyway and downstairs to a basement where they gym was situated. One senior lifter commented the gym was separate so that your screams couldn't be heard by the rest! I thought it was a joke, I was in for a shock!

Training consisted of strict lifts with a barbell. Clean and press, squats, dead lifts. Then you had to practise the two competitive lifts. The Snatch and the Clean and jerk. I found out straight away how weak my right leg was and I struggled terribly with my balance.

Competitive weight lifting requires great technique and balance and I had problems. Try as I might I just couldn't get the lifts right and a part of me was saying I don't really want to be doing this anyway. The sessions became a nightmare particularly if any of the seniors were training in the gym. They would deride sadistic pleasure from putting us youngsters through torturous routines. For example making you squat with a barbell until your legs were like jelly and you couldn't stand up properly. Even then they would make you carry on until you collapsed under the weight and they would just about snatch the bar off you. Also if you couldn't do a proper lift without dropping weight, they would put a heavy metal collar from the end of a bar behind you on the mat. You were then informed that if you fell backwards with the weight you would crush your spine on the collar (wonderful). This of course spurred you on out of pure fear.

As you made your lift, unknown to you they would kick the collar away at the last moment, but us naïve boys didn't realise this.

Dennis entered me for a competition in Newport about 12 weeks into my training. I told him basically I was nowhere ready but he said it would be good experience. That coming week I had sleepless nights and come the weekend of the event I was a nervous wreck. The walk to the pick up point for the competition seemed one of the longest in my young life and when I arrived mercifully the event had been cancelled at the last moment, what a relief!

I decided there and then to tell Dennis I did not want to competitively weight lift but when I was sixteen years old in a few months I would return to body build. He realised my commitment to Martial Arts and said that it would be OK.

The Empire housed some weird and wonderful characters. Situated in a tough part of town most of the guys who went there were hardcore trainers. When I returned and could workout in the main gym I loved it. There were so many great people to give you help and advice, especially the old timers that would tell you many 'secrets' of their trade. This was all a learning time, the good and bad.

The gym was multi-cultural, but the 70's didn't carry the political correctness of today. Many an argument or brawl would break out in there, as well as constant piss-taking. It was an educational experience for a young sixteen-year-old! For all the bad vibes in the gym, the same faces always turned up and trained together.

From that time I became more and more interested in fitness and strength training and it set me off on a path that would run hand and hand with my Martial Arts training.

In this day and age of hi-tech and expensive health clubs, the Empire club still survives and I think anybody who took up fitness training in the 70's certainly trained there at one time or another. As well as going to the Empire, I was still practising Kung Fu with the same group of lads. I was working now and I could afford to visit the gym twice a week and also train in Kung Fu.

I'm afraid I left school under achieving just before my sixteenth birthday in the year of the Queen's Silver Jubilee 1977. I had no O levels or A levels so I was looking at a manual job. I didn't worry, I just got on with it, earned my weekly wage and went training, and life was simple at that stage. Incidentally I got my first job after being sent out of a class for fooling around. Whilst standing outside I decided to follow some lads on the way to the headmaster's office to meet a guy interviewing for some job vacancies. Ironically from this episode I got a job set up before leaving school. What a stroke of luck!

Just before I left school the Kung Fu lads said they had heard of a Taekwondo class opening in a part of Bristol called Clifton. They were going to check it out and see what it was like.
Taekwondo was beginning to emerge then in '76/'77 as the next big art. I had seen some demos of it on television and was impressed by its powerful and flashy kicks. (Again I was a young man with stars in his eyes!) The guys reported back, the class was good and the instructor said he would honour our present belt grades. So the next Friday evening we met up at the bus station and walked to the Victoria Room, Clifton for the class. The 'Vic Rooms' is a large ornamental building well known in Bristol with grand fountains and architecture outside the front of it. It seemed a strange venue for a Martial Arts class. The instructor was a young Korean, who I believe was studying at Bristol University. He was very good and I can still remember his high standards all these years on, unfortunately I do not remember his name. Although he had accepted our grades, we felt the others in the class resented the fact that we had just waltzed in. We were to find out later we were going to have to fight for respect.
Taekwondo was very different in its approach to what we see now. It was very traditional. Basics, Hyun's (katas), 3,2,1 step sparring and then free sparring. This was tough, no pads, no protection, just get in and start trading. We also did loads of exercises for leg strength and power. We would have to do lap after lap around this gymnasium with bunny hops and duck walks, interspersed with leap fogs and jumps over a partner's back. When you completed this then it was kick drills one after another. Front, side, round hook, spinning, jumping, crescent, etc, etc over and over.
Each class ended with free sparring. You would do this in lines. You face an opponent spar, then when called go back to your place in the line and move up one to the next opponent and so on.
As I mentioned some of these Taekwondo boys were out for blood and often drew it! But our previous training held up well and we used to bring in a few unorthodox moves from our Kung Fu to good effect!
I regularly came up against my Nemesis in the sparring. He as a big coloured lad, who hardly ever spoke a word. He would impassively wait in line to spar. Everytime I closed in on him he would spear me on the end of a wicked front kick, with the biggest feet imaginable. This always reminded me of the scene in Bruce Lee's 'Game of Death' film, where he fights Kareem Abul Jabber, the huge basketball player. Kareem hits Bruce with a front kick in the chest when he approaches him, leaving a large footprint on his

yellow tracksuit, luckily I was still wearing my black Kung Fu uniform! Each week he would catch and hurt me and I would go away planning revenge for the next week. What really pissed me off was each time he caught me I saw the glimmer of a smile on his lips and I didn't like that. I must admit I struggled with the high kicks in Taekwondo. One reason was as usual, the right leg. Balance and power were still a problem and I mainly supported my weight on the left leg all the time. The second reason I began to question in my mind could I really pull some of these flashy kicks off in real life? The question for the moment was left un-answered. One of my best kicks at the time, though, was a spinning back kick. I could deliver this one hard and fast. I decided this was my weapon to beat 'Big Foot'.
Next time we sparred I deliberately let him catch me with his trademark front kick to drop his guard. As I moved in again I saw him cocking the kick and that's when I dropped in my spinning back kick. It landed fast and hard and my Nemesis fell to the floor faster than Emile Heskey being tackled! He lay there with a look of pain and surprise on his face. I must admit I thought he was going to get up and go berserk. But no, he did regain his feet and congratulate me and after shook hands. I had earned his respect and we became friends. Infact all the Kung Fu lads after about 3 months of hard fighting at the end of the classes had been accepted, we were in and I stayed with the class for 12 months before something else began to beckon me and grab my attention. Not another Martial Arts Style but the dangerous combination of girls and alcohol!

"Real strength is internal not external."

Chapter 4

'The Aikido Years'

I finally left the Taekwondo class, as my misgivings about the system came to a head. I felt slightly sad about leaving behind some good mates but I felt there was so much more out there in the Martial Arts world and I needed to discover it.

Again I was without any club but I carried on training myself and avidly read any material I could get my hands on concerning Martial Arts.

I still went to the Empire and I also attended a local youth club (Remember those?). At the club I played many sports from football to table tennis. Also I did a small bit of boxing. Nothing formal. There was a cardboard box full of old lace up boxing gloves in a cupboard at the club and my mates and me persuaded the youth leader to let us use them.

Each week he would monitor boxing matches in a backroom between us. It was all very crude and normally ended up with a free for all and everybody wrestling on the deck.

I can remember when the youth leader himself boxed with my mate Rob and Rob was taking a bit of a beating, so on an unspoken signal the rest of us jumped the Youth leader and gave it to him! For all the messing around I did enjoy boxing and it would play a bigger part in my training.

When I started work I befriended a guy called Alan who at the time was in his 20's. He looked after me and became a mentor in various matters in my life. He had been a bit of a tearaway in his younger years and had been part of a motorcycle gang. When I met him he was a lot calmer after getting engaged to a girl who worked in the office above the warehouse where we worked.

I used to talk about Martial Arts and Alan always said that it wasn't real fighting. We used to argue and it always ended up with a bit of a light-hearted scrap. Nearly every day we'd end up rolling about but it was usually pretty much in good humour. One day I remember whilst working, Alan grabbed me from behind in a bear hug over pinning my arms. He was a lot bigger and stronger than I was and I struggled to break out as he lifted me off the floor. In a desperate bid to break free, I got the soles of my feet up against the wall and pushed back hard.

He flew back quickly, losing his balance and crashed hard to the stone floor with me on top of him.

I immediately spun free as his grip loosened and went to pin him down, when I noticed he wasn't moving he was spark out! Shit, I panicked. Suddenly he woke up with a stare and I was so glad to see him awake, what a relief. You think we would have learnt our lesson but the next day we were at it again.

Alan was a great friend. He helped me with work, gave me sound advice on life and a whole host of dirty fighting tricks for emergencies. Out of work I also had become friends with an ex-school colleague. Our history was a strange one together. We first met in Primary School and for the first four or five weeks of meeting up we beat ten bells out of each other every playtime! Don't ask me why? He took an instant dislike to me (amazing) and I just fought back. His name was Shaun. Also of Irish decent. It got so bad our parents had to intervene and try and make peace, which they did and that was the end of the matter.

We grew up through primary and then Secondary together. We weren't really mates but reasonably friendly towards each other. Then, in one of the last school teams, a bunch of us were fooling around together and totally by accident I threw over a wall a stone which hit Shaun on the head. He did have a bad temper at times and he just went ballistic! I really was sorry and attempted to apologise as he came storming around from behind the wall. He piled in and started swinging punches at my head. I just froze with shock and he hit me un-answered a dozen times or more until some other lads pulled him away. I tell you I had more lumps on my head than a 'picnic' bar! I began to know how Humpty Dumpty felt! I had a job to rest my head on the pillow to sleep for a week! When we left school the incident had been forgotten and not long after his mum suddenly died. Living so near my mum suggested I go around to his house, as he might need some company. I really didn't want to do this but in the end I made my way there. When I went into his house we both felt awkward. But once we broke the ice, things got better. We started going out and about and within three months we were the best of buddies.

It was on his suggestion we tried a local Martial Arts club called the 'BRISTOL BUDOKAN' and investigated an art called Aikido. This was around 1978. Aikido was pretty much an obscure art and not too much was known about it, particularly from my point of view.

Shaun raved on about how he saw footage of a demonstration on television and had seen these guys effortlessly throwing each other around.

He was dead keen, I still wasn't convinced, and I wanted to carry on pursuing the punching and kicking arts. Anyway he finally persuaded me to give it a go.

The Bristol Budokan was a legendary dojo in our town. I hadn't really noticed it before, yet it was only 15 minutes walk from my house. It was a large, odd-shaped red brick building, three stories high. The building itself was quite old. Originally it was the humble base of the then fledging company 'Kleaneaze'. Then it become the Bristol Boys Five Club before a Ray Jenkins bought the building in the early 70's. Ray was a good Judo man and so is his whole family. Various members of his family are still practising and teaching Judo today at another 'Budokan' in Backwell near Bristol.

The building was purely for Martial Arts. Judo, Karate and Aikido. It had three matted floors. Small rest area, toilets and showers. In the 70's it was heaving every night. Again nearly everybody who practised Martial Arts in Bristol one time or another trained at the Budokan. Little did I know but the 'Budokan' would become on and off my spiritual home for many years to come.

The first day Shaun and myself walked in it was quiet, being a Saturday morning. The place smelt of sweat and feet (a typical Dojo). It was basic, spartan but an ideal place to train.

The first floor was empty, on climbing the second floor we saw a children's Judo class in operation. We asked the instructor if the Aikido class was on and he pointed upstairs. We turned to climb the stairs to the top floor, (shades of Game of Death again!). When we reached the top floor we saw half a dozen guys training. A small red haired man broke away from the class and came and introduced himself as John. He told us he was looking after the class whilst the chief instructor was in the States. He went on to explain about Aikido and invited us onto the mats to give it a try. Leaving our shoes and socks at the mats edge on we went for our first taster of Aikido. God, I was a disaster! It all felt so strange and different to what I had been used to before. I felt like I had two left feet and two right arms! We were shown classic Aikido techniques, which any Aikidoists out there will know with their eyes shut. Shihonage, Kotegeishi, Nikkyo etc etc. I struggled to get to grips with the subtle balance breaking, leverage and locks. At the end of the session my brain had gone into over-load and I'm sure John, the instructor thought we would never return. I was all for leaving it, but Shaun again convinced me to give it a month and see how I felt. There was another full class on the Tuesday and we agreed to go again.

The Tuesday class was busier and I was glad to note we weren't the only novices. Alan Drysdale the chief instructor was back and John assisted him. We got on better, not an overnight success, mind you, but then again anybody who has trained in Aikido will know it's not the easiest of arts to pick up straight away.

The small red haired man, John Bennett gave us great encouragement. John was a straight talker, a man's man. He was then in his mid 30's. An ex-Judo man, who had also done his stint of national service. John became a massive influence on my life, a good friend and ended up my best man at my wedding years later.

Around this time I will admit my training became a little erratic. The urges to go out, chase girls and have a few beers were strong. It did disrupt my training and although I never gave it up, I did miss weeks at a time in pursuit of other pleasures and this pattern carried on for about two years.

Shaun and myself if we had missed training in the week would go to the 'Budokan' on a Saturday morning and workout on an empty mat. Going through the Aikido moves, bits of Kung Fu and Taekwondo and now and again learning a bit of Judo from a guy called Bob who was one of Ray Jenkins black belts.

One morning I asked Shaun for a sparring match. The last time we had fought was in that one sided fight in the school playground. I guess I hadn't really got over it and knew I now had the confidence and skill to get revenge! Yes, I battered him, unmercilessly until he asked me to stop. Suddenly I was overcome with guilt looking at my mate in a heap on the floor and I picked him up and from that day on we never seriously fought again.

We went back and done our month and then we done another. Although I kept up my punching and kicking I was beginning to enjoy the close quarter techniques of Aikido and a few things were now beginning to make sense.

John Bennett had inherited the class as Alan had left to live in the States. This was good for me, as I loved John's approach to teaching. He enjoyed the whole art of Aikido but he did like to emphasise the more practical applications and that was right up my street.

Another John, who was of Polish descent, also assisted the class. I can't even begin to think of his surname, let alone spell it, but he went on in years to be a well-known figure in the Aikido world. He preferred the more flowing and Ki energy aspects of Aikido, so the two Johns were really chalk and cheese, but at least you got to experience the complete art.

The classes were quite small and soon Shaun and myself became regulars. It was nice to be part of a smaller group rather than just a face in a crowd, which I felt I had been in previous clubs.

Around this time we were asked to help run a local Youth club in the area. Earlier I mentioned I had been part of one for some years. This club was for younger children and the two young ladies that ran it needed help with the boys. Some were getting out of hand and bored and needed some direction. We were asked if we could help. I immediately accepted the offer as I fancied one of the young ladies who ran the club. Her name was Tina and through time with a little bit of messing about here and there, I finally plucked up the courage to ask her out. Doing this was harder than any sparring match I had been in, I can tell you! She was older than me by nearly three years and at first didn't think she'd be interested. But when she said yes, I was gob-smacked. This was the start of a great relationship. We weren't just girlfriend and boyfriend, we were soul mates, kindred spirits and good friends. The relationship would blossom into marriage and we are still together, still great mates after some twenty years now. (Wow that's some time). When we were going out together I was training three times a week and as our relationship became more serious, Tina decided if she wanted to see more of me she would have to join the Aikido class. Which she did. Initially she admitted it was just to see me for another night but in the end she became hooked on Martial Arts too and became a very competent exponent herself.

Being the only woman in the class, she learnt to look after herself quickly and having been a bit of a 'Tomboy' in her childhood, she adapted well. Soon she was just treated like one of the lads and she could give as good as she got (I can testify to this, first hand!).

So I was a happy lad. I was training now harder and more dedicated than ever.

I had a girlfriend who also trained and understood my passion for Martial Arts. What more could you need? Excellent.

Around 1980, John told us we were going to join the club to the BRITISH AIKIDO FEDERATION. This federation was run by the Japanese, it was the Uyeshiba style of Aikido. Morihei Uyeshiba was the founder of Aikido and although he had passed on his son had taken over the mantle. The BAF had direct lineage back to him at the Honbu HQ in Japan.

When we joined we were exposed to some of the best Aikidoists in the world.

I was fortunate over the years to train with many great instructors, Japanese and European and learnt much.

The system was very traditional. The syllabus was in Japanese and you had to learn to decipher it and speak it as well as practising the techniques. In our class the only time you spoke English was 'hello', at the start and 'goodbye' at the end. It was extremely difficult and now seems so un-necessary. The belt system was also traditional. White belt until you obtained black and the ceremonial hakama (split Japanese skirt).

When you went on a seminar there would be loads of white belts on the mat. Some could have been practising months, others years, you had a job to initially know.

In Aikido training your first techniques are learnt from wrist grabs. This we were told was because you could detect a person's experience by their grip. If it was weak or tentative they were a beginner. If it was strong and confident, the person was an advanced practitioner. I found this a good method, although I also found most black belts would treat you like a 5-year-old child if you weren't wearing a black belt as well.

We trained hard in this system, eager to be accepted and recognised. The leader of the BAF in England was Kanetsuka Sensei. He was a superb Aikido man. I first encountered him on a weekend course at Leicester in 1980 and was amazed by his speed, power and also grace of technique. Up to this point I hadn't seen Aikido at this level and I knew I had much to learn. Over the next three years I learnt plenty.

I was training three times a week religiously and going away on seminars nearly every other weekend. I travelled the length and breadth of Britain training. I trained in Oxford at Kanetsuka's private Dojo. I attended National and International courses and experienced the best in the Aikido world.

Any of you reading this book that has practised Aikido will know the names of the following and recognise them as great Aikido men. William Smith, Gordon Jones, Terry Ezara, Tony Cassells, Mike Narey and so many more whose names I can't recall. I also was fortunate to train under about a dozen Japanese instructors on some memorable seminars and some greats like Chiba, Saito, Tamura and Chibata, absolute monsters of the Aikido world.

Those of you who have read my other books will have heard me speak about Chiba Sensei. This man was/is a Martial Arts phenomenon, a true Budo Master and a Samurai placed in the 20th century.

Anybody who is anybody in the Aikido world will know Chiba. Normally people's faces drain of blood when he is mentioned and then there will be a story to tell. I managed to train under this legend on only a couple on occasions as he had moved from the UK to the USA. He was also recovering from a back injury from which doctors had said he would not train again. Needless to say he did and he would visit Britain a few times a year. When I saw him in action, John my instructor informed me he wasn't as fast as he used to be. Bloody hell! He looked a blur to me. If you can visualise Steven Seagel's Aikido in his films and crank it up ten fold we might be getting near! He was awesome for such a little man. When he arrived on the mats he seemed to grow and send a shock wave through the crowds.

When he first came to Britain he had a fearsome reputation. In his classes, broken bones and blood on the mats were not unusual. On most large seminars the Dan grades would proudly kneel at the front of the rows, waiting to be picked by the instructor to be their Uke (a receiver of technique). When Chiba was the guest instructor, they visibly shrank inside themselves and tried to make themselves invisible! When Chiba pointed to one of them and grunted a command you could see them inwardly groan, as they knew they were in for a hard time.

I have heard countless tales about this man. About the time two muggers decided to attack him as he came out of a railway station and steal his briefcase. He left them both rolling on the floor with broken bones. Or the occasion when giving a demonstration, he turned to speak to the crowd and his young and foolish Uke decided to tap him on the head with his bokken (wooden practise sword). Chiba instantly spun around outraged and knocked him out. Also a humorous tale about the time when he sat in kneeling posture waiting over an hour for his class members to arrive. When they eventually strolled in late, he couldn't understand why they weren't hurrying.

He angrily confronted the instructor and was informed the clocks had gone back an hour the previous evening. Being relatively new to England he hadn't known this. The tales go on and on. I witnessed first hand on a course how he made Kanetsuka Sensei look like a novice when he practised drills and techniques with him. It was a hugely humbling experience.

Although he had a reputation as being hard and harsh on his black belts, he was immensely gentle and controlled with the lower grades (I appreciated that at the time!). The sign of a true Master.

I only wished I had been able to learn more under him, but the chances were few and far between. His Aikido to me was the real Aikido. He had learnt directly from the founder Uyeshiba. Although people's images of Uyeshiba may be as an old man with a white beard, in his younger age his own Aikido was extremely powerful and rigorous. Obviously in his 80's he had to adapt and soften the practise.

One of Chiba's English instructors was William Smith. This man also had a tremendous influence on my training and me. He came from Birmingham and ran the Midlands Aikido. He was an extremely powerful and Dynamic Aikido man and a pure gentleman. He even apologised when he hit you, which was quite often!

He again was everything I thought a true Martial Artist should be and more. On the mat he was very powerful but as a teacher caring and always had time to help or talk to you, the same off the mat. I graded to my green belt under him and I owed him so much. Although I have lost touch over the years, Tina and myself think and speak of him fondly with upmost respect.

I had personally progressed immensely in the couple of years I had now been training in Aikido. I had not only experienced Uyeshiba style but also Tomiki, which is a sporting version of Aikido, which includes Randori against knife attacks. I can remember training in a class and competing as a young buck with testosterone flowing and beating everybody in sight, I loved it, but I'm not so sure about my opponents.

I also trained in Yoshinkan style, which was used by the Japanese police for control and restraint. This style is very direct and practical. I had so many experiences at this time, sitting here now I have a job to recall them all. I do know I was going through a 'proving' stage of my career and would go anywhere and train with anyone and mix it with just about everybody. I did become a bit of a bully and I didn't have time for whingers or wasters. My motto was if you are on the mats and you've got the belt then you take what's coming. Mind you I never dished out anything I couldn't handle myself.

I was used as Uke and bounced all over the place by many top instructions and I thrived on it. Some of the Japanese Sensei really twisted your joints and threw you over with ferocious power but I would always bounce back like the proverbial rubber ball. I was lighter and leaner in those days and very quick so I just took what they dished out.

Sometimes I was told off or admonished for fighting on the mats or being excessive, but I was only looking after myself. If anybody came to train at our class at the Budokan and I thought they were a bit cocky, I was over there and ready to prove a point.
In Aikido you trained not only in open hand technique but Jo staff and Bokken and I liked it all. I had some great battles and knocked people down and out with all the weapons. I played no favourites. Looking back it was just youth and you can't change what you have done. It was just the way it was at this time, but I may have been a bit tough on some of my partners. But let me emphasis in my defence, not against beginners or lower grades than myself.
I also hated politics in Martial Arts and how it controlled certain aspects of training. For example if you showed your face at the right seminar or summer school training camp you were almost guaranteed your belt promotion, whether you were worthy of it or not. I also despised the idea of honorary Dan grades. Individuals who were awarded their black belt because they were of some financial importance to the Association, or they were Goffa's with brown tongues that happened to be in the right place at the right time. Fuck'em.
I couldn't get my head around the fact that others and myself were training hard and long through the grades and these people were just given them. If I was on a seminar and spotted one of these said people I would 'home' in on them and if they were actually training (which was a rarity) I would start sharing some of my pain with them, I just couldn't help myself! I saw the grading system clearly in black and white with no shades of grey whatsoever.
Other pet hates were some Dan grades treating lower grades like they were imbeciles.
I would sometimes partner one who would presume I was a complete novice and start explaining a technique in language a four year old child would understand and then show me how wonderful they were by cranking the technique on me! I would wait patiently for the immortal words, 'you try it not', and then I would go into turbo drive, smashing the technique on hard and fast. I loved to see the smug expression on their face change to ones of horror and pain! A Dan grade is a measurement of your skills and certainly to be respected but respect is like a girdle it stretches both ways and as a high grade you shouldn't assume you are God and everyone else is inferior physically or mentally. That's a bad mistake and one I've seen made umpteen times by instructors that are so wrapped up in their self importance they disappear up their own asses! Hey don't get me started on this subject.

Anyway by this time in my training my mate Shaun had left but Tina was there with me and going strong, in more ways than one. We were engaged to be married and on the August 14th 1982 we were. As mentioned John Bennett my instructor was my best man. He had become a valued friend and mentor and kept me on the right Martial Arts path and gave me sound advice.

You can tell how fanatical I was on training. The Friday night before the wedding on the Saturday which is usually the groom's stag night I went training! Another instructor Mike Narey who had come down from the Midlands was taking the class and was under strict instructions not to use me as an uke, as nobody wanted me turning up at the alter the next day with a black eye or arm in plaster! I of course didn't know this and was progressively getting more frustrated throughout the evening as he hadn't called me up for our ritual 'bashing around'. Five minutes from the end of the class he did call me up and gently showed a few throws, I was miffed. Only after class did he tell me what had been going on and we laughed. I was so young at the time I didn't see any dangers whatsoever. Anyway I made it to the altar in one piece and have been married over 20 years. Some people say that I got married young and maybe I did but I was really happy with the way my life was heading and had a girl who not only loved me but understood me and could have a 'bit of a scrap' I was in heaven, why spoil it, I missed out on nothing and don't regret a thing. I had two or three years of fooling about before meeting Tina and it wasn't anything special, I can take it or leave it, most of the time its all bullshit.

I'm glad I chose the path I did. Also now at forty-one years old I have done most things in life but lot earlier so I am reaping the benefits now. I am not up to my neck in a mortgage, bills or nappies and we are getting our own lives back. Plus I am young enough and 'handsome enough' to enjoy it.

If I'm asked how I like to unwind, then I have no better pleasure than after a hard week of training, teaching and working than sitting at home with my feet up with my wife and children around and a cold bottle of beer in my hand watching T.V. Simple pleasure, yes, but absolutely priceless.

I have many mixed memories about my later Aikido training. The good things were the comradeship that built up in our small club and the support we gave each other. Bad things, dreaded politics, internal bickering and power struggles.

A lot of special training sessions stick out in my mind. Going over to Cardiff to train on a blazing hot Saturday with Shibata Sensei, who was visiting for the weekend.

I went alone and eventually tracked down the club by asking a policeman directions. (Now there's a novelty a 'Bobby' on the beat) The club was in a disused warehouse in a decidedly dodgy area! We trained upstairs on a matted area and the session was going to be videoed. Along with the outside temperature being about 85 degrees, the sun beating relentlessly on the corrugated iron roof of the building there were two large powerful lights focussed on the mat for filming. Boy, did I sweat, that session. Shibita was a powerful Aikido man and we trained hard and fast. The canvas mat area was soaked with sweat, you could have wrung a pint of water out of my heavy judo gi, but what a memorable session. Travelling back to Bristol by train I sat slumped in my seat, gulping bottled water to pacify my thirst, I was severely dehydrated and aching all over but what a fantastic day. I sweated off about four pounds and at that time I couldn't afford to lose it.

Another session that stays in memory was the other end of the scale from scorching hot to absolutely freezing.

Occasionally we would travel to a club in the Forest of Dean (Wales). This dojo was a long prefab type of building on the edge of the forest itself. We always seemed to visit in the winter when the Forest was picturesque with the trees covered in snow or frost. The dojo though was absolutely sub zero. You had to train excessively hard to melt the frost on the windows and soften the mats up.

Although your body eventually warmed up your fingers and toes stayed as cold as icebergs. Not ideal if you jarred them or if they got trampled on. As the steam from our bodies warmed the atmosphere, the doors would be opened and the watery winter sun would filter in, giving a golden hue to the mat. It was still bloody cold and those Welsh boys were tough buggers. Happy days!

As mentioned earlier I trained under Kanetsuka Sensei on many occasions, but his training changed drastically over the years. When I first met him he showed fantastic Aikido technique but gradually he changed and showed less and less. Instead he made you do endless cuts with a suburi bokken (heavy wooden sword for developing grips and forearm strength) over and over again in kneeling or low squatting postures until you lost all feeling in your lower legs and would keel over.

Sometimes he would check your balance and posture by whacking you on the back with a bamboo kendo shinia. Also we did loads of suwariwaza (traditional Japanese kneeeling techniques), doing two-hour sessions without getting to your feet.

This was bad enough on the canvas mat where you would burn layer after layer of skin off your feet and knees, but I also did this more than once with him on a wooden floor (extremely painful).

We found out later he had been diagnosed with cancer and I think it just changed his whole concept of Aikido practise. Thankfully he got over this illness.

But although the latter type of training developed tremendous character and spirit, it didn't do anything for my technique or progression. In the end these relentless sessions just became survival and mental strength. This type of training would eventually lead to my disenchantment with the whole Aikido scene after nearly 5 years training, in which for political red tape I was still only graded to green belt. Because I would not pay the money to go on the summer schools or Easter courses, I was getting overlooked. Kanetsuka played his favourites and if your face didn't fit you weren't going to progress. Don't get me wrong I wasn't the best of Aikidiosts but after training, as long and hard as I did for those five years I certainly deserved to have progressed further. I know some people who have achieved a black belt within two years! Although gradings weren't the be all and end all for me when I was on seminars I saw people around me with high grades that didn't have half my ability. Maybe because I didn't bow down to political pressure I stayed where I was. But that's me, I've been like that in many areas of my life and probably held myself back because of it.

One hilarious memory, which didn't seem quite so funny at the time, was when I went to do a demonstration of Aikido with Sensei Mike Narey. I loved working with Mike. I would throw the attacks in hard and he would bounce me around. A perfect combination.

I toured around Bristol and Wales with him on and off over 6 months with Mike using me to promote and demonstrate Aikido. This particular night we went to an evening class centre to give a demo. Mike had rang up earlier in the day and asked if they had mats, to which they replied 'Yes'. So we were all set.

Entering the room, we found that they had plenty of mats. The only problem being they were the type of mat you put down in front of the fire-side at home.

I protested to Mike I wasn't falling on them but some how he persuaded me. We overlapped as many as we could and he done the demo. I was thrown from pillar to post, sometimes landing on the mats sometimes not. The watching group must have thought I was crazy (maybe I was).

Afterwards I was black and blue and Mike said "Well I think that went off okay". Fucking unbelievable! Mike is still around now training in Bristol and recently recovered from a heart attack. He was out for a while but is back on the mats teaching. I liked and respected him a lot, we had some fun times together.

These are just a handful of incidents from these years. I did so many training sessions, courses and demonstrations I just can't recall them all. But I had gathered a wealth of experience and knowledge. My training in Aikido really came to a head when we invited Kanetsuka Sensei down to Bristol for a weekend training course and grading. I had been training for my 2nd kyu blue belt. At the end of the second days training, John brought forward to Sensei our licenses and he looked at them to see who had passed us on our previous grades.

He then looked up and told us we were all going for high grades within Aikido and this weekend he thought we couldn't do our basics let alone attempt anything advanced. He asked us to think seriously about whether we were ready for this grade and he called for a 15-minute time out. Again frustration set in for us. Everytime we seemed to be making a progress we just got knocked back. It had been like this for every grading. I personally was at the end of my patience and told John I thought we were being treated badly and it wasn't right, Tina voiced the same opinion as did many others waiting to grade. John knew things had come to a head. We returned to the mat and Sensei called first John up to grade. I must say here that John Bennett was an absolute stalwart for Aikido and as my instructor first class. He had trained so hard and was only going for his first brown belt grading after having relinquished all past grades on joining the BAF and wanting to start with us from the bottom.

When John stood up on this seminar infront of about 70 people I had no idea what he was going to do. He rose and said, 'Sensei I have thought long and hard about what you have said and I have decided not be grade. Kanetsuka was shocked and implored John to grade. But he was adamant and walked forward to retrieve his license. This spurred me and others to follow and claim our license as well. We just lined up and took them back. Kanetsuka was speechless.

Only Polish John decided to grade and successfully passed his brown belt, maybe we would of as well, who knows? We all left the mat and I personally never trained with Kanetsuka or the BAF again.

I knew now our club would be splintered and it would never be the same again. I felt great loyalty to John but I also knew it was time to move on and explore pastures new. The grading incident had been the straw that broke the camel's back, but there had been other issues as well.
I'm a practical man and loved the combat side of training and in the past year that was missing. I was young, eager, fit and wanted to test myself so I had to leave.
Telling John this was one of the toughest things I ever had to do and I agonised over it, he had become such a good friend and the club was like a close knit family. I was about to lose that identity and comfort zone and go out on my own, it was scary but also exciting.
John understood. He didn't want me to go but he couldn't hold me. It was a sad day for Tina and myself. John respected me for coming and telling him to his face, instead of just disappearing. I wouldn't have done this anyway I had too much respect for him and that's why now I like people to speak face to face with me if they have any problems in my classes.
So the Aikido journey was over. Five full and totally committed years. It took some guts to drop five years training and start afresh but I had been taught much I was no longer a raw beginner.
The best things I personally took from my Aikido experience were great self-discipline, respect and spirit. These things I have never lost and would need for the next leg of my journey.

"Traditional Martial Arts has given me discipline and respect, two admiral qualities"

Chapter 5
'Tracking down Ju-Jutsu'

As I have already mentioned I loved the practical aspect of Martial Arts and as a young man it was extremely important to feel that I could handle myself if needed.

I had begun to have reservations about my Aikido training effectiveness on many occasions before I finally left training.

Once I recall a conversation in the pub I overheard between my instructor John and a guy that had recently started training. He was a good lad, but he also had had some real street fighting experiences. He asked John how he thought his Aikido may hold up against a boxer in a fight? John replied that he thought a good boxer would probably be too much for the Aikido man, as he didn't practice against boxing punches. I was gutted. Here I was training hard with belief in what I did and then I heard this. I thought to myself, well this isn't good enough, you need to know how to handle a boxer, your chosen art should have the answers. I had always had an open mind to Martial Arts and had accumulated a great number of books on the subject, exploring all avenues. I knew there was much more to discover.

Also I had concerns over the effectiveness of the techniques in the street. I had witnessed over the years many fights kick off and none and I mean none had the ritualised movements of Martial Artists. It was all fast, explosive and scrappy, ending up usually with both participants rolling on the floor. Aikido was a good Martial Art but it wasn't giving me the answers I needed.

I realised on reflection I had got caught up in the whole spectrum of the Aiki world and had forgotten my basic interest. Effective fighting technique.

As mentioned during the Aikido years I still kept my interest in the punching and kicking arts. I was keen as ever on boxing and watched avidly some of the best fighters of that time on T.V. Big names like Hearns, Hagler, Leonard, Duran, Holmes, Aurgella, Pryor, McCallum and Chevez. I not only watched but also studied their technique.

I also had an interest in Ju Jutsu, one that had been with me on and off for some years. I first saw Ju Jutsu techniques in a magazine in the late 70's.

Each month this magazine would have colour step by step photo strips of Ju Jutsu techniques demonstrated by Robert Clark, Richard Morris, John Steadman, Charles Allmark and Eric Marshall.

At that time I had no idea who these famous Ju-Jutsu greats were. I was more interested then in Kung Fu. But later when I got into Aikido I went back and studied these magazines and saw some similarities in the arts. The Ju-Justu techniques seemed much more complete, with each move starting with Atemi-waza (vital point striking) then a throw and take down followed by some amazing joint locks or strangles.

To me, in that moment I realised this was the missing link I had been looking for up to now. That blend of striking and grappling art together. I began to seek out more knowledge about these great Masters who really had been responsible for Ju Jutsu's re-birth in the UK during the earlier 70's. I managed to find some good Ju Jutsu books, which just wetted my appetite for the art, and when I finally left Aikido I knew where I was heading. I needed to find a Ju Jutsu class as soon as possible.

For a few months I was in limbo and found it strange not to be training, but I am not one for letting the grass grow! I sent off for a Martial Arts directory so I could scan the area for a Ju Jutsu class. When the directory arrived and I read through it I discovered there were no clubs near Bristol. The nearest was a club in Taunton, which is about 50 miles away. Their classes were on an evening and it just made it impossible to get there after a day's work and fighting rush hour traffic.

I then spotted a Ju Jutsu club in London run by a Sensei Del Connelly. I had never heard of this man before but I decided to write him a letter and explain my situation.

A few days later I received a reply. He said that I was welcome to visit his club on a weekend and train free of charge. Sensei Connelly informed me if this helped me into the Martial Art of Ju Jutsu then he was happy to do this for me.

This was great, so the following weekend Tina and myself along with two other lads, who had decided to leave Aikido, Brian Barker and Mark Fortune, we headed by train to London. We got connecting tubes to East Ham and tracked down the club.

Sensei Connelly warmly greeted us and showed us into his Dojo. It was a smashing place. It had a large matted area, rows of punch bags and a small rest area. Over a mug of tea we chatted and he told us the day was ours and he would show us whatever we liked.

Sensei Connelly was a 3rd Dan under Professor Richard Morris of the British Ju Jutsu Association, whom I had read a lot about.

We were taken through some of the BJJA syllabus. I loved the freedom of being able to use strikes and combine these with much closer body contact throws than I had been used to in Aikido. Also the ground work and floor pins were excellent.

There was a young lad training who was a yellow belt. Sensei Connelly demonstrated techniques with him. This lad's standard was excellent and I was told he had been practising a couple of years. I mentally made a note if I was as good as this lad in two years I would be happy. Later some others arrived to train. There was one big guy who was a black belt in Kyokushin Karate and he introduced me to low leg kicks, leg blocks and shin roundhouse kicks. My legs were black and blue after half an hour. We then moved onto the bags and went through kicking and striking drills. Later we practised ground grappling.

Coming from five years of very traditional training, this relaxed and open style was a breath of fresh air, plus it felt like I had the leash let off and could explore whatever I wanted. I loved every minute.

At the end of the day we thanked Sensei Connelly for a wonderful time, he had been true to his word. He had showed us a wide range of skills and hadn't charged us a penny. He was a first class Ju Jutsu man and I haven't forgotten the generosity he showed me all those years ago around 1982.

Travelling back on the train, although we were all tired we couldn't stop talking about the day. My mind was absolutely racing with ideas, I was totally committed to developing the stuff we had learnt and I know my long term goal was to open a Ju Jutsu class in Bristol and eventually teach this art. I was a man on a mission. But as they say Rome wasn't built in a day!

When we returned we decided as a group to find somewhere to train as soon as possible. Brian came up with a room at a Community centre in an area of Bristol called Stockwood. We clubbed together and bought some cheap mats and we were off!

We could only get the room once a week, so every Tuesday from 7:00pm to 10:00pm the four of us trained working on Ju Jutsu technique, boxing, grappling and basically pooling our knowledge together. It was a time of experiment and it was embryonic stages of the Ju Jutsu I would eventually teach.

A few weeks after our London trip I had a letter from another instructor a Sensei Mike Marshall, who was based in Southampton, he asked if we wanted to come down to train and see what his system was about. We were all up for this, so we made the trip.
I didn't realise at the time but Sensei Marshall would figure highly in my Martial Arts career for the next few years.

"Who said Ju Jutsu was a Gentle Art?"

Chapter 6

'The wild bunch'

Sensei Mike Marshall was to say the least a bit of a maverick. He was unconventional in what he did, but I enjoyed my time associated with him.

His Ju Jutsu was different to what I had previously experienced up to then. Most of it was basic and simple, with the emphasis on being workable. The reason for this was that Mike had taught his Ju Jutsu and close quarter combat to HM Special Forces. He had been a member of the famed S.B.S as well as having worked as a bodyguard.

We all enjoyed our days training and I got on well with Mike and his people. We had gone through a lot of technique and training and had given a good account of ourselves, so we were invited to join Mike's Association, which we accepted.

Mike ran two Associations. The first was the Japanese Ju Jutsu Association, which taught pure combat Ju Jutsu. Mike's father who had trained in Japan and learnt this Ju Jutsu there had passed down the Association to him. The other was the Great Britain All Styles Self Defence Association (GBASSDA). This was an umbrella association where all styles of Martial Arts would come together to teach and train in the self-defence and combative elements of their choosen system. It was a big melting pot to exchange ideas and techniques and it worked very well.

GBASSDA was an early pioneering association for later one's like the British Combat Association and Self-Defence Federation. Although now in this day and age we have many Multi-Styled organisations, back then in the earlier 80's this was something new and radical. I was glad to be part of all of it, I gained a lot of experience during my time with them.

GBASSDA was made up of some weird and wonderful characters. The good, the bad and the mad (all were ugly anyway). You had to sort the wheat from the chaff, so to speak, until you came across some hidden jewels.

Mike Marshall was an off the wall character whose past and experiences were shrouded in a bit of a mystery. Then there was 'Mad dog' Dave Vincent and 'mad' Micky Upham two Ju Jutsu men from Liverpool. Typical scousers, hard training, hard living guys with a great sense of humour. I went on to train with both of these men some years later.

We also had Dave Turton one of the most experienced and knowledgeable combat men in the UK today. Dave still remains a good and much respected mate of mine. He is known for his no-nonsense approach to training and his hard edge. Back then his edge was a lot harder and his training sessions were tough. He taught his Goshinwai Combat, not only unarmed skills but single and double sticks, Yawara Bo, fighting knives and a whole host of makeshift weaponry.

Another good mate was John McCartney from Belfast, Northern Ireland. He was another enigma. His lads and him would travel over to England by boat for every National Course and would be decked out in camouflage and black woolly hats! He was doorman in Belfast but in the past had worked as a mercenary fighting in the then named Rhodesia in South Africa. His system of CQC was very hard and brutal.

Next up was John Sheridan and Mike Middleton of the Aikido research federation. Both were good Aiki men schooled also in Aikijutsu and Hakka Ryu Ju Jutsu. They asked me on more than one occasion to grade for my black belt in Aikido. But I turned it down as I felt to me I would be going back in time and not forward.

Last, but not least was my now good friend Jamie O'Keefe an East End Cockney lad. Back then he was a young, lean and mean Karate man who gave out respect to a chosen few. He would arrive alone at courses and was very capable, confident and outspoken about what he felt worked and what didn't, and quite rightly so, as he did it well. He thought nothing of walking into a place full of Ju-Jitsu, Aikido, and practitioners of other arts, being the only Karate guy in a venue knowing it was full of everything but Londoners, or Karate fans.

This was at the height of a very political time between all arts and the ridiculous North-South divide that some believed existed. Jamie was a natural observation expert, which he now refers to as 'people watching'. He could, within minutes, differentiate between talent and bullshit and deal with either according to how it was offered out. He is no different now apart from being larger, and has become a renowned self-protection instructor, educator and author of numerous books on the subject. He also owns and runs New Breed Publications, which have published all my books to present date.

Jamie is a very knowledgeable man on the self-protection scene after having worked in front line security for many years. Having said all that I'm still better looking than he is, although he won't admit it!

There were others also in the Association but I just can't recall their names. It really was a band of mavericks, renegades and misfits but hell we had some fun! The original Dirty Dozen.

So after joining up and receiving our memberships we began to work hard on the syllabus determined to get our grades. I did want to open a class as soon as possible but I wanted the proper grades and official backing before I did this.

We would travel whenever we could down to Southampton to train with Mike and attend National seminars in Birmingham. Between this we just kept our private training going together.

The Community centre where we trained had plans for expansion, so they wanted more space. The space being the back rooms where we trained. That was not good news for us.

After some persuasion they took half of our room and built a partition wall for us to train behind. It was really weird, us one side belting the hell out of each other and on the other side would be people sat drinking or playing pool in a bar like environment.

We didn't care though, nothing would get in the way of training. We worked hard and when we travelled up to the next National course we were informed that we would be grading.

Tina, Brian, Mark and myself went into a room in front of the grading panel and were examined. Sometime later we emerged, Tina and myself with 1st Dan black belts and Brian and Mark with brown belts, what a result! We had all trained extremely hard for this and we just didn't put a foot wrong, we turned it on and breezed through the grading. I believe that preparation is everything no matter what you are attempting to achieve. Our preparation had been first class. We were fit, strong, conditioned to last the pace and we had rigorously gone over and over the techniques until they were second nature, nothing was left to chance and that's how we had succeeded.

I was over the moon with my grade but Tina's had been extra special, she was the first lady in GBASSDA to be awarded a Dan grade and she had earned it the hard way, no quarter asked or given. Her performance had been faultless.

One moment that sticks out in my mind and Tina and myself still laugh about it, was when we had to perform knife defences. Mike handed me a knife in a leather sheath. As I went to take it out I noticed how difficult it was to extract from this sheath. Finally I pulled it free and lunged in a thrust toward Tina. Mike stood up in alarm and yelled out to stop but by then Tina had deflected my hand and had taken me over in a vicious wristlock and disarmed me! Mike and the panel looked ashen faced.

He said ‘We normally keep the knife in the sheath for safety. We just wanted you to feel the weight of a real blade!’ We just looked at each other; we had trained with ‘live’ weapons before so you could appreciate distance etc. This practise must always be done extremely carefully and only when you have the skill to do so. On that day of the grading we hadn’t given it a second thought!

We travelled home again that night tired but happy. I told the others it was time to open up the club to the public, we were now ready. So around about 1984/85 the first class of the Bristol Goshin Jutsu Combat Academy opened up, although at the time we were called the Bristol Self Defence Academy.

We now had the main hall at the Community Centre with lots more room. We initially had about 12 to 20 people show up to train. Looking back then the training and the teaching was a little raw, but I was learning my trade all the time.

I didn’t have the luxury of a full-time Sensei living on my doorstep. I had to do a lot of things in trial and error fashion. I would travel when I could to increase my knowledge but for the most part I developed my clubs in Bristol here through my own tenacity and will to succeed. Tina, Brian and Mark had given me great support but at the end of the day it was my name advertised as the instructor and I ultimately carried responsibility.

The class at this time consisted of three hours. The first hour would solely be down to exercise and conditioning and I did ‘beast’ people. The training was without compromise, last men standing sort of stuff.

I used to bring along to the class a large ‘masterblaster’ and play through a tape both sides while we did the exercises. Starjumps jump squats, burpees, squat thrusts, pushups, sit-ups, leg raises, jumping squats etc etc etc.

I remember one guy who had joined the class say to me after struggling through the Bruce Springsteen tape ‘Born in the USA’, “When I listen to that fucking tape next time It wont ever be the same to me again!”

After the warm-up, two hours of Ju Jutsu, Self-defence and sparring methods would be practised. Students came and went but gradually I built up a little hard core following.

I had some lean times at the class with three or four people turning up, sometimes on other occasions the hall was full! The training was hard and it didn’t allow for different ages or fitness levels. It was very much take it or leave it sort of stuff. I was still developing myself and following a certain path and those who wanted to come along for the ride could.

A year later I graded for my Second Dan under Mike Marshall and Dave Turton. Brian also gained his first Dan. Mark had unfortunately left us and Tina's training had been cut short because she was expecting our first child.

Motherhood takes up a lot of your time and it certainly changes your life forever. We have three children all told. At this time present they are aged as follows. Thomas, 16, Jacob, 14 and Lauren, 11. They are all great kids and they all are pretty handy at Ju Jutsu themselves. A dynasty for the future? Who knows, we shall see.

Tina never really got back into training after the births of our children. She did help me with numerous ladies Self-defence courses and she keeps fit now by going to the gym and aerobics. She still can handle herself mind you, but back then she was a very capable martial artist.

Brian went on to be a very loyal and trusted instructor with me. He never let me down. He was always there with help and advice. Brian supported every class, travelled with me on seminars, and was my uke for demonstration and so much more. He was thirty-five years old when he started Martial arts and was in his early forties when the classes were really taking off. He had a catalogue of injuries during his training. A double hernia op, broken collar bone and chronic rheumatoid arthritis in his wrist joints these were just a few of his problems. His doctor had told him on more than one occasion to give up Ju Jutsu, but he kept on training, until the pain in his joints got too much. At this time I didn't realise how hard it must have been for him to keep training the way he did. I was in my twenties and training like a lunatic, it's not until these days that I can appreciate the calibre of the man to keep up with being my training partner through some very, very hard sessions. He finally retired from the Martial arts and is living a life of luxury touring around and staying in Europe. Good for him, he was a very good friend and a strong and trust-worthy man, I owe him much.

From the hard-core group of student's came other guys who would go on to gain their black belts under me. Noticeable, Martin Williams, Neil Bartlett and Mike Griffin. All good Martial artists but different in their approach and techniques. These guys emerged at a time where the word was getting around about my Ju Jutsu and the profile of the club was getting better.

I decided it was time to open another class and returned to the Bristol Budokan. It was inevitable I would return again to my old club. I started back then on a Thursday evening and that night became a special class especially for all our senior grades.

There was nothing better in years to come to see a mat full of blue, brown and black belts having a really hard training session. It was great to see and I was proud to have taught these guys.

I was around 23 years old when these two clubs were running. Things were busy, what with a job working from 8:00am to 5:00pm in a timber yard/saw mill down at the Bristol Docks, helping bring up a young family, sleepless nights and trying to keep my training going! Tina was very understanding and knew my passions for the clubs, she supported me and gave me no hassle when I went out to teach or train. This helped me immensely.

I was still regularly travelling to train with Mike Marshall and by then I had also joined his Japanese Ju Jutsu Association. I was eventually over the next few years graded to first Dan in Japanese Ju Jutsu and Atemi Ju Jutsu, which was a great honour. I had come so far so fast and I had learnt so much. Mike also schooled me in C.Q.B techniques of the Special Forces unarmed and with stick, yawara-bo and knife. The yawara-bo is a small stick-like weapon, the original forerunner of the kubotan. It can be used to strike, lock, restrain and manipulate pressure points. Instructor's back then would graphically show you its effectiveness by striking you without reserve and crushing your bones. I have been hit on the arms, legs and body to collapse and have had bruises on my bruises. I once done five-hour instructors course with this weapon and had a job to move the next day. I recall a certain Mr.Turton being particularly vicious with the yawara-bo.

By 1988 the GBASSDA began to fall apart. Major players were leaving like Upham, Turton and O'Keefe, the great originals were now failing. I just think we all came as far as we could with the Association and it was time to move on.

I stayed another while but decided I had reached a learning curve and I needed to expand my horizons again, so at the end of 1988 I left. Mike wasn't too happy originally but in the end relented and let me go.

I think it wasn't long after that GBASSDA came to its natural end. I lost track of Mike and have never spoken to him again. If you're still out there Mike and you just happen to read this book, many thanks I enjoyed my time with you I learnt much.

After leaving GBASSDA I still, liked to go different seminars and keep an open mind. I enjoyed a great few seminars under Professor Brian Dossett of Spirit Combat International. Here is another Martial Arts maverick that burnt his 5th Dan black belt in front of the WJJA panel and left to form his own Association. They said he wouldn't last, oh how he proved them wrong.

Professor Dossett had his many critics but I enjoyed every training session with him. His down to earth cockney approach is unique and for a man of great talent he has no edge or ego.
I attended many of his B and D combat courses in his Middlesex Dojo. These courses were open to Martial artists, bouncers, bodyguards and fighters of every ilk. The courses advert read 'no cry babies please' so you knew you weren't in for a picnic.
I recall two other instructors, the mighty Tom Baldwin an extremely powerful Ju Jutsu man and CQC expert Gary Stringer. Along with Prof. Dossett we trained in hard street combat techniques, grappling and no holds barred type fight were everything was all in and you just had a good tear up. It was rough and ready and I suppose you had to be slightly mad to participate. Again I met some crazy people and would be Bruce Lees! They were soon exposed though when the training began in earness.
I was just a face in a small crowd and Brian Dossett would not remember my name or me but I remember him and look back with mixed memories of fondness and fear at those great sessions. If you didn't walk away from one of these crazy classes with a bloodied nose, thick lip or bruised ribs then you had escaped a minor miracle. I can remember waiting on the mat's edge with a mixture of excitement in my body doing battle with my stomach churning in knots. It's a bit like queuing up for a wild roller coaster ride, part of you wants to experience it and part of you doesn't. I suppose it's got to be done!

'I could see further by standing on the shoulders of giants'

Chapter 7

'The Micky Upham Experience'

On a few of the GBASSDA'S National Courses I had witnessed the skills of Micky Upham. Mike Marshall had always told me if I ever got the opportunity I should train with this man. So when I left GBASSDA I decided to see if I could track him down. Elusive or what? This guy was harder to trace than Lord Lucan!

I enquired through some of the instructors who were in GBASSDA but with no luck. Then one month I was flicking through 'Fighters' magazine and saw an advert for Mick's Goshin Ryu International Association. Bingo, there was an address. So I wrote a letter explaining who I was and that I would like to join his Association and train under him.

Now I believe this was the one and only time Mick ever advertised in the Martial Arts Magazines and I just happened to read that particular issue. I do believe in fate and this certainly was a case of it.

I had heard much about Mick Upham. That he was an elusive character and that he didn't take in outsiders to his clubs. He ran a tight ship with a small group of clubs in the native Liverpool area. He referred to them as his 'warriors' or 'army'. I had also heard some pretty 'hairy' things about Mick and that he sailed a 'little close to the breeze', but this still wouldn't put me off, I was desperate to learn from this guy.

Micky is a unique man. A crazy scouser, with a great sense of humour, a little seen gentleness and balls that come in a dumper truck! On the mats he is perpetual motion! Himself and his Uke 'little Mike' were a great double act together. Their demonstrations of Combat Ju Jutsu were fantastic with sound effects and crazy antics thrown in, I loved it. Mick was a demon Martial Artist. He had the hand speed of a pro boxer, the kicking ability of a top Taekwondo performer backed up with the grappling and throwing skills of Ju Jutsu. He was something special. I have never seen a better combat Ju Jutsu man and that is with no disrespect to those I have learnt off of over the years. Mick is a one off and when I first met him I realised I had made contact with somebody who would again influence my Martial Arts training.

I received a reply to my letter and Mick said that he would accept my club into his Association. In the letter I asked if Brian and myself could come up to Liverpool to grade under him. Mick agreed to have us up and take a look at what we could do.

We drove to Seaforth just outside Liverpool and waited in a designated pub car park for Mick to arrive. Finally he did arrive, with a quick handshake and a few words, he asked us to follow him and we drove to his Dojo.

When we arrived Mick explained about his style and philosophy on the fighting arts. His outlook was 100% practical. He said he could show us all the classical and fancy Ju Jutsu or could show us the 'real stuff'. We settled for the latter!

First he took us through a grading. He fired technique after technique at us, throws, locks, chokes, self-defence, ground grappling, weapons. We just kept going at a terrific pace for an hour or more. Then he showed us some of his methods of Ju Jutsu.

The 'Goshin' system he taught was stripped to the bone of any unnecessary movements or over complicated technique. Short, sharp and powerful Ju Jutsu at its best. Brian and me trained hard in the new methods and at the end of the day I was awarded my third Dan black belt and Brian his second Dan.

Mick organised the certification and even had them counter signed by Soke Brian Walsh 10th Dan one of his old instructors. I believe Soke Walsh is the highest graded Ju Jutsu man in the U.K. He is based in Liverpool.

Returning to Bristol we worked hard on modifying our Ju Jutsu and began to streamline it, so it became sharper. Both the clubs were doing really well and I felt at long last I was reaching some of the long-term goals I had set myself.

My relationship with Mick Upham was a strange one. I couldn't really refer to him as my Sensei because he used to seemingly disappear off the face of the earth for months and then re-appear. I also got Mick down to the Budokan here in Bristol two or three times. But once more I would piece the training together myself from whatever I had been given and just carried on. Even under Mick I carried on my open-minded practice and went to train on other seminars.

I travelled to stoke to train and also to teach on the Bushi Kempo Ju Jutsu Association national courses. I met and got to know Sensei David Hand, who was a gentleman on and off the mat and also acquainted Shihan Peter Browne. Both these men ran this Association. I enjoyed the freedom of just being able to train and have a good bunch of lads with me.

I laugh now when I recall us all clambering into a venture-scout mini bus that we would hire cheap to go on seminars! How the thing got us to the venues I'll never know. It coughed and spluttered its way along and I wonder what people thought when it pulled up outside a seminar venue and we all climbed out! It was just like 'Del Boy's' three wheeler! They were good days and learning ones.

I also managed to train on large seminars under Robert Clark and Richard Morris two of the most senior Ju Jutsu men in the country and I even attended a Ninjutsu seminar under Brian McCarthy, the very well known and respected exponent of this art.

This seminar I remember well as we were the only group outside of Ninjutsu that showed up to train and I think some of there lads thought they could have a bit of fun with us. Wrong! We certainly held our own and dished a bit out. On this seminar was supposedly the cream of the UK Ninjutsu world but we weren't phased by that. Guy's like Martin Williams, Neil Bartlett, Mike Griffin, Andy Loxley and Bob Kingdon were hardcore students and would go anywhere and give me 100% no questions asked.

I recall I had broken my big toe a week prior to that seminar and to say it was sore was putting it mildly. At the start of this seminar we had to do lots of partner drills, very gymnastic like. One drill was to make a human pyramid. Yes, starting with four men on the bottom standing, then three would climb up on their shoulder's then two on to theirs and finally one little guy at the top. I'm not a great one for heights and had to climb to the top! I usually get a nosebleed changing a light bulb! I tell you I was all over the place and ended up jumping down. Then I was on the bottom row of a decidedly shaky foundation. All was going ok, until the guy next to me stood on my broken toe and I jumped a mile causing the whole pyramid to collapse in a heap! It was a weird and wonderful day. Mc Carthy was very good at what he done but I personally didn't rate anybody else.

My 3rd Dan was achieved in 1988, this gave me the authority to grade students up to 1st Dan. Martin Williams, Neil Bartlett and Mike Griffin became my first generation of black belts behind the original founder members. None of them unfortunately train today!

Martin was a tall and powerful lad with great potential to become a very good instructor he had been with me since he was seventeen years old. He gave up training for the love of a woman (poor lad) and I lost track of him until he turned up on my fortieth party. I didn't at first recognise him because he was bald as a coot!

Infact I've seen more hair on a piece of bacon. Alas that's what the love of a good woman does for you.

Neil Bartlett was a superb Martial Artist. He stood about 5ft 3ins, but what a pocket dynamo, he was skilled in Ju Jutsu, Kempo and Muay Thai. A chronic injury to his back vertebrae put pay to his training and he now lives in New Zealand. I had many an adventure with Neil, he was as unpredictable and a funny guy.

'Mad' Mike Griffin came to me as a Ju Jutsu blue belt but got a bit of a culture shock when he saw how we trained. But he took to it like a duck to water. Mike was one of the toughest men I ever trained with. He was a PTI in the prison service and had had his share of real life drama. He had handled some dangerous inmates in his time including the Krays, Peter Sutcliffe and Charles Bronson.

He loved to train hard and him and me would have some infamous tear ups at the Thursday Night Budokan sessions. We would be training and sparring in all out bouts back then well before NHB events came into force. He was relentless and really pushed me hard in training. At his peak he was around 14 stone and was 6ft2inches, he was a bit of a monster and not many people liked training with him.

I have so many tales to tell about my times with him I could write a chapter just on this but here a few more of the best ones.

When he was taking his brown belt grading he was giving a torrid time. At the end he had to grapple two of us at once. This ended with him crashing into a group of other students who were also waiting to grade. Neil and me dived on Mike and we gave him another battering and he was doing his best to escape but I noticed that three of the lads waiting for grading were also pinning him down so he had no chance. He never realised this and after couldn't figure out how he didn't escape.

On his 1st Dan grading surprising nobody turned up to be his uke so surprisingly 'Muggins' was left to do it. Mike was hyped up like 'Gazza' at a FA cup final. His adrenaline was running wild and I had to tell him on numerous occasions to control it. When we came to weapon defences I was on red alert as at black belt level we trained with live weapons. I can remember Mike disarming me of a small knife and pinned me to the floor holding the blade under my chin to finish. With his adrenaline flowing his hand shook and he stuck the knives tip into the fleshy side of my chin. First blood had been drawn!

We also drilled gun disarms against a replica blank-firing pistol. Mike once more disarmed me of the gun and had me pinned to the floor with it pressed to the side of my head. Yes he forgot it was loaded with blanks and pulled the trigger. I was deaf in one ear for days after. What a crazy man and a crazy grading.

Mike also had a habit of jumping out on people and surprising then very much like Peter Sellers in the Pink Panther films.

One day I was in town with Tina and I spotted him in a shop in Bristol's well-known Galleries Shopping Complex.

I told Tina to let me know when he was coming out of the shop and waited outside.

Bear in mind this is a Saturday afternoon and the place is crawling with shoppers and security. Mike come out of the shop and I jump on him. He thinks he's being mugged and starts fighting back hard before he realises it was me. "You bastard", he panted, "I was ready for you". "Yeh right" I replied. I'm surprised we weren't nabbed by security.

On another occasion we were coming back from a course. Mike was driving in one car and I was in another. We both pulled in to get some petrol at a motorway garage.

I was waiting in the passenger seat of the car whilst Martin who had drove filled it up. I suddenly looked up and saw Mike running across the forecourt with a police baton in his hand. He yanked open the door to get me out. I kicked out at him and grappled the baton away. He broke into hysterical laughter as he ran back to his car. God knows what the poor woman cashier thought who was watching the scene unfold from behind her till.

Mike and me done many seminars together over the years and he was a loyal friend and instructor. His job moves him around the country quite a bit and at present he is away and not training with me. He is a great character and we had some wild times together.

In 1992 I asked Mick Upham if I could grade for my 4th Dan. He informed me that nobody under him had ever received that grade and if I wanted to come up and try for it I could but he warned me it would be fucking hard.

I felt over the years that I had to prove myself to Mick. I'm sure he thought we were all southern softies down here in Bristol and didn't have the 'balls' for real training. Well I attempted to prove at every given opportunity that I did have the balls, spirit and resolve.

I knew the grade was going to be hard, so I started on a severe training regime of fitness to get myself in top shape. I was running, lifting weights, doing loads of callisthenics and Ju Jutsu training. At my work I was using shifting loads of timber, boards and doors as part of my fitness training. I was lifting heavy and carrying loads various distances as well as up flights of stairs punishing my body at every opportunity. In my dinner hours I would disappear upstairs in a part of the warehouse and bang out half an hour of press-ups, squats and sit-ups followed by going through all my strikes and kicks. I was like a man obsessed, I was totally focussed to get this grade and prove myself beyond doubt.

When the day arrived a mini busload of my students and me met Mick again just outside Liverpool and then followed him to an outdoor venue, which would be where the days training would take place.

This was to be one of Mick Upham's infamous "In the woods" seminar. I had been told about these before, where a bunch of unexpecting trainees would be brought out in the woods, 'beasted' and left to make there own way home or have their train or coach tickets ripped up and made to run home. I had been warned they weren't for the faint of heart and be prepared for anything.

As our mini bus pulled up behind Mick's car at the designated venue, I told all my people to pull out all the stops and give it 100%, they and me were on trial and we couldn't afford to fail. I looked around and saw looks of nervous apprehension on faces It was like a moment from one of those old black and white war films just as the platoon was getting ready to go over the top!

We followed Mick into the woods and walked along the trail. Although I was talking with him my eyes were peeled on the bushes and trees waiting for some kind of mad ambush.

Finally we came to a semi-clearing. A fine mist was rising off the grass and light drizzle was coming down. There in the clearing were Micks 'warriors', all warming up decked out in full camouflage gear and army boots. We all acknowledged each other and after a basic introduction, Mick told me I was going to be assessed throughout the whole days training. This meant for 5 hours I was going to be under the microscope. I would have to have 100% attention throughout and couldn't afford to lapse. After a brief warm up we started with Kempo strike combinations and Kotsu-ho-Jutsu (joint breaking and locking). We went through umpteen variations and then continued those with sweeps and reaps.

All the while the rain came down getting heavier. The woods were situated by the coast of Seaforth.

Mick was having fun by going around and setting off fire crackers and thunder flashes whilst we trained, it was like a bad day in Vietnam. Then came the marathon throwing session.

The ground was a mixture of sand, mud and bracken and it had become very wet and boggy. We began one for one throws, hip throws, hip wheels, body drop, sweeping loin, half shoulder, full shoulder, winding throw, leg throw, head throws etc, etc. Over and over we just kept banging them out. Mick making sure he gave me more and more throws to execute. Everytime you hit the floor you were getting wetter and wetter and the odd combat boot kicking your ribs or stamping your ear didn't exactly cheer up the proceedings! After a solid hour of throws we stopped for some lunch and a well needed drink. These sessions were sparten and nobody stopped for fluid unless instructed to do so.

When the break was over we started back with weapon defences and also using the short baton, Yawara Bo and flashlight as weapons. This was followed by groundwork combat styles. Grappling around in mud might make a great nights entertainment for some but when you are doing it yourself it is very tiring. I do admire those lady mud wrestlers, they must be fit.

Next I was taken with my partner Martin Williams to another area, with a stretch of clearing between the trees a couple of hundred feet long. A dozen or so of Micks boys accompanied us. We separated and faced our partners at either end of this course. Mike then announced it was stamina training time. He warned anyone who flagged or quit would have a long walk home. I looked up the course at Martin and knew as a young and fit black belt he would be with me all the way. Then we were off and running, literally. I first sprinted the course to Martin, he then threw me with five hip throws, we both hit the floor and done ten press ups and then sprinted back to the other end of the course where I threw him and we again done the press ups and so we went on and on, circuit after circuit. At one stage we were doing ten throws each and then twenty press-ups. Next came wheelbarrows on your knuckles, your partner guiding you down the course, you had to plough through whatever was on the floor, no questions asked. When you reached the end, ten push ups and then bring your partner back. This went on for what seemed eternity. Then it changed to worst torture! Piggy backs down the course, ten squats at the end with partner on your back, five hip throws and then your partner done it. This was excruciating. At this stage we had been going an hour non-stop.

I vividly remember as I was carrying Martin's 6ft1 inch and 13 stone frame down the track. Mick sat at the other end sipping on a can of lucazade and asking if I wanted to stop for a drink. I knew this was one of his devious ploys and I would shout out "No Sensei I'm fine". "Are you sure?" he would reply,"It's beautiful, ice cold". "No Sensei" I would again shout and go back up the course.

Next he would be jogging down next to you with a cup of warm tea telling me how wonderful it tasted and did I want a sip. This was all mind games. He would then start telling me how tired I looked how hot I was and that he didn't think I was going to make it. I just shut him out and gritted my teeth, inwardly thought, "You bastard".

Around this time everybody else joined the circuit for moral support and I must say my people male and female did me proud. We were now into body crawls, jump squats and duck walks up the course. At the end one person would lie down and execute 50 sit-ups then lift their legs off the floor 6 inches whilst partner would punch and palm slap them in the abdominals. Lovely stuff!

Near the end of this tortuous ninety-minute marathon some of Mick's men were flagging, a few falling to the floor totally exhausted and de-hydrated. Mick was screaming, "Get up you lazy bastards, you'll never train with me again". He was pulling guys up by their hair and pushing them back onto the courses.

Within all this there were still some moments of humour which I always love. At one stage I jumped up onto Martin's back and Mick was playing psychological games telling him he looked finished. This spurred Martin on into a new lease of life and he shot off down the course. Mick with a look of surprise on his face shouted out, "Bloody hell lad what are you a fucking gazelle".

Another one of my students said at one stage after a wheelbarrow walk he was doing push-ups and was on the urge of collapse. As he was sinking down towards the grass he spied a dog's turd directly in his eye line and this spurred him on to complete the rest of the exercises.

Finally Mick shouted out to stop. At this stage I had gone beyond fatigue and was de-hydrated badly.

Mick came up to me and said, "You know if you had stopped for a drink I would have failed you". I just nodded. He then shook my hand and said "Well done lad you've passed you are the first fourth Dan under me. You put some of my lads to shame. It was good".

I was elated but very tired. I remember being led back to the minibus between two others dehydration had cleared my sense of balance and my legs had disowned me, but I was grinning inanely.

We now had the long journey back to Bristol and Martin who had been my right hand man all day had to drive back. The bus was a wash with excited chatter and congratulations.
I just sat in the front passenger seat and soaked it all up. About an hour into the journey it had gone strangely quiet and I peered back over my shoulder to see everybody crashed out asleep. I smiled to myself, they had earned it and done me proud. Although I could have slept as well I kept my mate Martin company all the way home to Bristol.

I felt that day I had really come of age and had proven much not just to Mick but to myself. My physical and mental fitness had been tested and I had come through. It had been one of the toughest training sessions I had encountered but a few years previous I had prepared for this day with another extremely brutal and testing experience.

"Our greatest glory is not in never falling, but in rising every time we fall"

Chapter 8

'Tough training and new horizons'

Between the years of 1988 and 1992 although I associated and trained with Mike Upham on many occasions, I still went to other seminars and met new people one of these being Shihan Alan Tattersall of the then United Kingdom Ju jutsu Association.

Allan was a very experienced Ju Jutsu man originally gaining all his grades from Ju Jutsu great Professor Robert Clark. He went on to form the UKJJA which was based in Rochdale.

UKJJA ran some great seminars, which I attended regularly over the years and got to meet and train with the likes of Leon Jay, son of the legendary Wally Jay of small circle Ju Jutsu fame. Kirby Watson and Ian Griffiths of the Diato Ryu Aikijutsu. Trevor Roberts 'The Bolton Ironman', Peter Browne and many more. A wealth of experience, talent and varied training.

On one such weekend seminar in Sheffield 1989, I encountered one of the toughest training sessions I have ever experienced. This was with one of the visiting instructors from the Israeli -Anti- terrorist squad. He brought along with him his two sons, also instructors of CQC.

There were various mat areas with different instructors on each. All third Dan's and above were told to head for the Israeli's mat. So people like myself, Upham, Roberts, Browne and others were altogether.

This Israeli instructor without a doubt was a combat veteran. He had fought in the conflict of war and had killed. He was an expert in unarmed combat, knives and firearms as well as sentry removal skills and garrotting. He again had a presence about him that I hadn't felt often on the mats.

I think his sole aim for the day was to not only educating us in real world combat but also see what us British were made out of and how tough we were.

Israel had been a country in conflict for years and these guys skills were being put to the test on a regular basis, now it was our turn to be put to the test.

The instruction started with a brief demo of their combat skills and a lecture in broken English about what techniques work and those that don't under extreme pressure.

We ran through some of the moves, low kicks, palm heel, elbows, knees and sharp chokes and takedowns. Then we had to put these techniques into live sparring practice.

We just kept swapping partners, facing a new one and sparring, no pads, and no rules. I tell you it was unnerving and frightening. There was an extreme test of your 'bottle'. I don't mind admitting I was scared. A lot of the more classical Ju Jutsu Stylists struggled with this type of training. They were not used to the pressure of it all and I could clearly see some didn't like or agree with it.

The one thing I instantly noticed was that a lot of the fights ended up on the ground. Old news now to the initiated but back then in 1989 an eye opener. I got to have a bit of a 'play' with Mick Upham's right hand man 'little Mike' and we had a hard little scrap. I also went up against Mick himself and gave as good as I got. His kicking was fantastic though and my ears rang with a few good roundhouse kicks. Some people were getting lumps knocked off them and were visibly flagging.

Those who have read my book 'In your face' will know I ended up out in front of the class fighting one of the sons. It was all in except it was palm heel strikes to the head, not punching. We exchanged blows until I got caught in a standing guillotine choke and this Israeli whispering to me if I struggled he would break my neck. Deciding this might spoil my day I seized his testicles for a release, as this happened he raked at my eye and opened a cut up underneath it. The father broke it up and we went at it again, ending up in the assembled crowd. Again as we were separated. I must admit I had lost it slightly and fired a 'Judas punch' at the back of his head as I dived on him. It was broke up a final time and it was over.

Not long after we broke for dinner, I remember sitting in a toilet cubicle drenched in sweat, blood seeping from my eye and my forearms and shins bruised, thinking what the hell am I doing here. It was the aftermath affect of adrenaline and I felt bad.

When I joined the others for lunch many were complaining the training was too severe and dangerous. Some were not going back on the mat after the break; a few of these are big names in the Martial Arts today but shall remain anonymous. Mind you part of me wanted to go back to Bristol but I convinced myself it couldn't get any harder. What a fool I was!

After the break the sparring started again but this time two people would fight, then on a signal one would drop out and be replaced by a fresh opponent.

These were two minute bouts, that doesn't seem long until you experience all out no holds barred combat for that length of time over and over.

I remember I was up against this lady Aikiodist who had no punching or kicking skills. I was just keeping her at bay but then I was being urged to finish it, and the Israeli's and the assembled crowd vocally made it known to do her no favours.

This must have fired her up and she whizzed a sudden strike past my nose and then I went up a gear and fired a short roundhouse kick to her thigh and as her hands came down, dropped her with a palm heel to the face. No sooner done another guy launched himself on me, from the crowd and we were having a furious grapple on the floor. I eventually managed to get over the back of him whilst he was on all fours and drove a downward elbow between his shoulder blades. This took the fight out of him as I went for a choke. Then I was out and another took my place.

There were some brutal battles, none more than Mick Upham against Trevor Roberts. Brilliant stuff. I can remember Mick reversing a position on Trevor and was just getting off the floor when a change was called. Mick was off and I was back on again.

Now I was a young and up and coming instructor. Trevor Roberts was a Ju Jutsu legend and I don't expect for one minute he will remember this. As I was called out it was almost like I was in a dream. There was Trevor 'The Bolton Ironman' on all fours just about to rise. I thought there is no way I'm letting this bloke get to his feet. So I ran and launched myself in to mid-air, it seemed to take ages then I was on him. I gripped him in a side headlock And I suppose the scene resembled one of these Wild West rodeo cowboys hanging onto a wild steer (no offence meant Trevor) I just gripped on for dear life and rode out the storm until another change was called.

The finale to this part of the seminar were three people stood back to back in a triangle formation in the centre of the mat and the remaining 30 odd people ran in and just attacked them as one mass. Guess who was one of the three? Yep, yours truly.

Well we went down under an avalanche of bodies and I thought at one stage I was going to be crushed to death. Then pure survival instincts took over, these guys were playing for real and weren't going to relent. So I started butting, biting and gouging my way to freedom. There were screams and grunts as I went for it but I was on autopilot. I recall at one stage 'Little Mike' looming above me and attempting to strangle me, I just clamped down on his little finger with my teeth and I was away.

I managed to scramble to my feet, beaten but not bowed. It reminded me of surfacing from a long period of time under water, gulping for air and flapping around all over the place. Scary stuff.

The final part of training was specialise stuff. Prisoner restraint techniques, hog-tie-ups, sentry removal, knife combat, multiple opponent, firearm, disarms, garrotting techniques and combat ground grappling. I strongly suggest, never letting yourself be hog tied and carried around, not even in the privacy of your bedroom! It's a highly unpleasant experience, especially whilst lying helplessly, your 'so called mates' stick the boot in!

What a weekend end, this had been a seminar to put you fully to the test and I felt I had come through. I shook hands with the Israeli's at the end and they all signed a certificate for me. (No, not one for being criminally insane). I saw respect in their eyes and it was mutual. It had been an extreme test. The free fighting was just as hard if not more than what we see today in the mixed Martial arts arena, only back then some twelve years ago it was not for sport it had been for pure survival. Those memories I think will stay with me forever.

As mentioned the UKJJA hosted many great seminars, which I tried to attend as much as I could and still kept in touch with Mick Upham but our visits were getting fewer and fewer for reasons I don't really want to go into.

UKJJA were one of the first Martial Arts Associations in 1992 to bring in NVQ coaching certification. Alan Tattersall was a leading light in trying to get all instructors to attend special coaching courses.

Most sports at this time had taken on board NVQ coaching, but the Martial Arts were a grey area, was it a sport? Some practised it as just self-defence as traditional art with no sporting application so how could all the rules, regulations and guide lines apply to it.

It was a time of uncertainty. Instructors with ten, twenty or thirty year's experiences were arguing the point "What can I be taught" I have been running clubs successfully for years. I have official grade certification what more do I need? I don't need some sports coach coming in and telling me how I should teach? There was lots of unrest and bad feeling.

I attended an initial meeting at the UKJJA HQ in Rochdale and listened to the arguments for and against. I could understand both points of view but at the time, the bottom line was eventually all instructors would have to have NVQ coaching certification or they would find it hard to teach in any public building.

By this time my original class had now moved to a new venue at Whitchurch sports centre and I was concerned that if I didn't have the appropriate certification I would be pushed out. So I decided that I would attend the seminars and Brian agreed to also do this.

So we went on weekend courses at the Rochdale HQ and a Mr Tony Gummerson, a well-known and respected sports coach took them. The courses weren't about how to teach Martial Arts, we had all been in the game long enough to do this. Topics covered were how to set targets and plan training, working with children or disabled. Counselling students over training set backs and injuries, nutrition, fitness, managing a club, organising events, training safety, coaches responsibility, how to deal with emergencies, first aid etc etc.

For all my misgivings, the courses were really interesting and in the long run they certainly made me a better coach and run a more professional set up.

Exams were done in written form and also practical demonstration. You were also given workbooks to take away and implement certain principles and techniques into your classes and get feed back from the coaches who would monitor and assess your ability.

After around about a year I received NVQ level certification in the following: Assistant coach, Club coach, Coach level and Senior coach level all endorsed by the National Ju Jutsu Council and signed by Alan Tattersall and Tony Gummerson. This certification added a lot of weight to my other grade certification and certainly gave me more experience in the world of coaching Martial Arts.

I still kept my travels going around the UK and bring my guys to train with anybody I felt I could learn from.

Between 1992 and 1994 I travelled regularly and enjoyed some odd training. Highlights I remembered are training with Master Larry Tatum of American Kempo system. Master Tatum's speed of hand was awesome and his combination strikes were blindly fast. A powerful Martial Artist but a true gent. I also got Mater Bob Rose 6th Dan in Kempo down to Bristol. This man is a great character, because of Native American blood in him he fought in two tours of Vietnam, trained under Ed Parker, Larry Tatum and knew stars like Elvis Presley and Charles Bronson. Through the Kempo scene he had seen and done just about everything you could in the Martial Arts world. Fantastic character and I enjoyed not only his training but also his 'War stories'.

I attended a seminar in 1993 in Coventry run by the International Martial arts Federation and got a chance to train with the great Japanese Ju-Jutsu Master. Shizyka Saito. This gentleman was getting on in years but he was technically brilliant and still powerful. He chose me on a few occasions to demonstrate his technique and I felt those powers first hand.

My first taste of Brazilian Ju Jutsu can again on a seminar hosted by Peter Browne. Franco Vacirea a Brazilian based in Switzerland came to London. Along with his brother he showed some amazing ground skills and first class instruction. I don't think the assembled crowd really appreciated what they were taught. Although I already had read about Brazilian Ju Jutsu and the Gracie family and I fully enjoyed my first introduction into this fascinating art.

I again got a taste of Martial Arts Israeli style when Krav Maga expert Eyol Yanilov came to Bristol. Ironically the Bristol

course was held at Lifestyles fitness centre which in years to come would become one of my permanent and most popular class venues.

When I turned up for their course, there was only a handful of people there to train. How crazy, a world renowned instructor on the doorstep and not for the first time Bristol was sleeping. Their loss, my gain, Krav Maga was a military based system that was then taught to civilians for self-defence. The defence is based on quick, sharp and straightforward techniques. Simply in nature highly practical. We trained in multiple drills, good practical stuff backed up by Eyol Yanilov's world wide knowledge of his first hand experience of self-defence, having worked in security in some of the most dangerous countries in the world. Highly enjoyable training and stone's throw from where I was living. This would not be the last time I trained in Krav Maga and it was nice to know that this man had heard of my name in Britain and had went out of his way to, give me personal instruction and advice.

The late, great Gary Spiers was another man I got to train under on his special applied street Karate seminars. These seminars were always lively with plenty of workable technique and sage advice from a man, who was the Godfather of front line security for over 35 years. This man stories of his real world experience were worth the asking price of the seminars alone. Although I didn't personally know Gary I was greatly surprised and saddened by his untimely death. He was a man who literally cheated death on many occasions and seemed virtually bullet proof. He was a big man big man, not only in physique, that will be sadly missed.

I treasure some of the gems of wisdom he left from those seminars. I hope his full life story will be told one day, so he can he remembered for the great Martial Artist he surely was.

More courses and training were to come my way. As 1995 began to loom, I didn't realise that this year would change my life considerably and set me on my life time ambition to become a professional full time instructor.

'Be not afraid of growing slowly, be afraid of standing still'

Chapter 9

Beginning of a life time ambition

At the start of 1995 I was determined to try and expand my classes and also my profile. I felt there were a lot of people out there who would be interested in training in my combat Ju Jutsu but weren't aware of the club or myself. So I set out to try and rectify this, but I found that being stuck in an 8.00 to 5.00 job day in day out wasn't giving me the time to do what I wanted to do.

I had been working in timber yards and sawmills most of my life and although I was a qualified sawyer and also yard foreman the job was beginning to get me down and I had lost all enthusiasm for it. There were many reasons for this but basically lack of staff, wage cuts and consent hassle from the management were all taking their toll, on top of this having a young family and family responsibilities, plus my heavy training regimes.

Something had to change. I had set myself a massive work ethic and I was in danger of being swallowed up by it all.

I had a bit of a shock when I went for a routine health check and the doctor found my blood pressure was a little too high. I went back the next week and still it was the same. Now for somebody who has prided himself in being super-fit this really did trouble me. I knew I ate pretty sensibly. I didn't smoke I drank little and didn't use salt or eat over highly quantities of fat. When I sat down and analysed my present life style it was stress that was the factor. It can creep up on you, no wonder it's called the 'Silent killer'. Duties, responsibilities at work home and training, plus lack of sleep due to the kids and basically running around like a blue ass fly hadn't helped.

I knew something had to give, this had been a gradual build up and now I had to readdress the balance. Once I was aware of the problem I soon got it under control and the blood pressure went back to being normal by itself.

This and my gradual dislike for the job prompted me to see if there was life beyond the gates of the timber yard. I had always dreamt of teaching Martial Arts for a living and I decided this was the best time. I had the necessary qualifications and experience and I felt the time was right.

I was thirty-three years old and I felt I was nearing my peak and didn't want to leave it another five years and then regret it.

I set the wheels in motion by contacting some of the local Sports centres and asked if they would be interested in a Ju Jutsu coach and a self-protection instructor.

I met with the managers and brought my CV, trying to convince them that what I taught was different to kick boxing or Taekwondo.

A few months earlier with the help of a contact I had made my first training video for my grading syllabus. My good mate and fellow black belt Andy Wintle transferred a short montage of this onto another tape and I brought this with me and asked each manager to view it and then make their decision. This all took many weeks to arrange meetings and sort out details but in the end I secured work at three more Bristol based Sports centres and was employed by the Bristol City Council as a Martial Arts/Self Protection coach.

It was a start but it wasn't going to give me a massive income to support my family so I devised a plan to ask my manager at the timber yard if I could step down from my job as foreman and take a part time post. The only reason I though he might go for this was first, Andy was willing to step into the foreman's job and secondly the manager used to practise Karate and often spoke about Martial Arts to me and he knew my passion.

After consulting head office, he went for the idea and I was on a three-day week, giving me two days off to promote and expand my Martial Arts business. At first it was hard and Tina and me struggled for money, having to cut back on a lot of things and tread water for months. I'm sure our parents would have helped but we were too proud for that. Tina supported me every inch of the way and never once doubted me, even when I began to doubt myself. She would encourage me and fire me up and never let me be down for long, what a lady. I gradually got the three new clubs up and running and all you instructors out there will know how hard that an be, the work and planning that needs to go into this area to make it be successful or for the first few months trying to make it pay. In the mean time I was writing letter after letter or phoning different Associations, group's etc asking if they wanted self-defence training during the day. Once more I had many knock backs and then gradually I got a few requests. The hard part of any business is getting your foot in the door. Once that is achieved, I feel the best advertisement is word of mouth and a testimony from somebody. This is how it went for month after month, gradually building and relentlessly never taking the foot off the pedal.

Tenacity can knock down walls and I was beginning to develop this by the bucket load!

At this time I also began to develop my writing interest. I first started writing articles and sending them off to Martial Arts magazines. In the beginning I had little success and then gradually one or two were published.

Steve Grayston's Martial Arts was the first publication to give me regular space. I am extremely grateful to Steve for his help on setting me off on the road to exploring bigger and better writing projects. Getting established is hard work and you just have to have dogged persistence. You have to get the publishers and editors to know your work and also know your credentials as they receive bucket loads of articles everyday, so you have to rise above the mainstream. Paul Clifton of Combat, Bob Sykes of Martial Arts Illustrated, the great Terry O'Neil of Fighting Arts International all gave me space in their publication. But Tim Ayling of 'Fighters' has been an incredibly loyal supporter of my writing for many years and has done me proud.

I haven't been paid for any article in Martial Arts publications but it's like free advertisement for your system, club or products that you sell and this has helped me immensely in raising my profile and developing my business.

Also at this point I must mention Geoff Thompson, self-protection pioneer and prolific author who gave me much advice, help and guidance and used his influence to help open a few doors for me. More coming soon about how I first met Geoff and why I'm proud to call him a good mate.

I also started to make more training videos on different aspects of my art. These are not BBC Broadcast quality but good enough and reasonably priced for people to learn form. They have all been very successful particularly the 'Impact Ju Jutsu Series' which has sold really well.

The videos have sold not just in the UK and also Europe and further afield. I have received some really positive and complimentary comments from people, who have purchased them, including many high graded Martial Artists, which is always nice. I have produced along with Andy Wintle, who is a first class cameraman, nine videos to date and there might be another one or two in the pipeline. I always enjoy making the videos but they are hard work. Firstly you have to plan it, write, choreograph it, direct it and also be in it, no mean feat. I also like to thank all my 'lads' who have appeared in the videos and made them the success they are.

Next I began to plan a book. I had been an avid reader of Martial Arts books for years and had built up a vast library. With the help of two brilliant specialists in rare and interesting books, Mr John Sparkes and my old pal Mr Tony Downing I have managed over the years to purchase many diverse publications. These guys are simply the best at what they do and nine times out of ten they will come up trumps for you.

I had an idea to write a book on self-defence for the smaller person because there was no text solely addressed to the problem. Myself being below average height had trained with taller and bigger people all my life. I had developed techniques and strategies to combat a large assailant and I felt this would be a different type of book that hadn't been covered before.

I spoke with Tony Downing about the idea and he assured me nothing had been written on the subject and I should go for it before somebody else took the idea.

So I began the project and worked whenever possible to get my ideas down on paper. Sometimes I would sit up to the small hours of the morning writing and in the long run it all paid off.

Now writing a book can be a problem in itself but trying to get somebody to publish it is an even bigger headache. Believe me it can deflate your ego and self-belief in seconds.

I wrote countless letters to every publisher under the sun. I used to go into Waterstones bookstore and take the addresses of every Martial Arts publication house. I bought the 'Writers handbook' to find more addresses and editors actual names so I could address my letters personally to them.

Rejection! Rejection! Rejection! No one wanted to know, or wanted to take a risk on it. I really didn't think I would get any interest. Then you start questioning the book and wondering is it any good anyway and what made you think you could get a book published in the first place. It became a big psychology battle and it's very difficult to keep upbeat about the whole thing.

I had first toyed with the book and began to write notes around 1992. It was now speeding towards the end of 1995 and still I was having no luck with publication. Once again I put the idea on the back burner whilst I pursued other things. Then out of the blue I got a break!

I was reading through one of the latest Martial Arts magazines when I came across an advert for new book release, the title intrigued me. It was called 'Dogs don't know Kung fu' looking closer I saw that the author was Jamie O' Keefe, now there was a name from the past.

I ordered the book and enclosed a letter reminding Jamie of our connection in the early 80's with GBASSDA. Jamie was pleased to hear from me and said I should call him to discuss what I thought of his book.

I phoned and he told me he had just started up his own publishing company, NEW BREED based on the success of 'Dogs don't know kung fu'. I seized the opportunity and asked him if he would look over my manuscript for my proposed book. Jamie agreed and I sent it off.

Within a few days Jamie rang me and told me he thought the manuscript would make a great book. So that was that, the wheels were beginning to turn for my ambition of getting my first book published.

I sorted out the finer details with Jamie and he then set about getting my book "I thought you'd be bigger" into print.

I really enjoyed this period of time and learnt so much about the book publishing business and work entailed.

Jamie worked professionally and tirelessly to give me help and advice and slowly the project came together.

Just before Christmas 1997 the book was ready. Jamie, who was travelling down to the south-west, came and delivered the first print personally to my door. It was great to see the first copy and also my old friend in person.

Although Jamie had done the entire computer work, scanning and printing, I was proud of the fact that everything in the book had been done by me. All the texts, all the illustrations and the entire photography arrangements and photo placement. There is a real feeling of achievement when you see a project go through from a bundle of hand-written notes to emerge as a complete book with your name on it.

This started a long and continuing partnership with New Breed and Jamie. He has helped publish my other books as well. "In your face" "Grappling with reality" and my latest in the latter part of 2001 "Bad to the bone."

From 1997 to 2001 I had written four books, more than I could have hoped for plus this one obviously. They have all sold well and although I am certainly not a Frederick Forsyth or Stephen King, I am pleased with my achievements. It had always been a dream of mine and I had fulfilled that dream and not many people get to do this.

New Breed has gone on to greater success, having published many more books on the cutting edge of Self Protection and Martial Arts and Jamie has been a positive stepping stone for many new

authors. I highly recommend you checkout New Breed or if you have a serious book project in mind speak to Jamie. He is the only person I know that insists that you keep 100% of your copyright and you keep all the money you make from selling your book.
He will not allow any contracts to exist apart from trust, so you can leave New Breed whenever you want and owe nothing. He has set up New Breed a stepping stone to help authors with unusual projects and ideas.

As a finish to this subject, book writing and article writing is not easy. You learn and develop as you go along and you have got to be prepared to spend many hours planning and writing. I have done all my work without the aid of a computer. Jamie has often joked that I write my books with chisel and stone and to be honest its not been far removed from that. I've hand written all the manuscripts and Tina has typed them. Old fashioned to some, maybe, but it shows with the will to succeed you can achieve anything you want. As for computers I've just managed to understand the workings of a calculator, but I have plans on that front for the future.

'The man who won't read is no better than the man who can't read'

Chapter 10

'Keep on moving'

Along with the first book in 1997, I also was still keen to further my abilities as a Martial Artist and keep making a success of my ever-expanding clubs.

I now had a new hard core section of people training and they were to become my third generation of black belts. Great guys like Rob Cannon, Matt Sperring, Paul Flett, Andy Wintle and Phil Davies were all going to be heading for black belts in the next few years to come and become extremely good Martial Artists and highly valued members of my Bristol Goshin Ju Jutsu combat academy.

For now I was again seeking new instruction. I hadn't heard from Mike Upham for sometime so I thought I would seek out his old partner Dave Vincent. Dave had been a close pal of Mike's and helped develop the Goshin style of Ju Jutsu in the Liverpool area, but in recent years they had split up. Dave now had his own Association named the British Kempo Ju Jutsu union.

I contacted Dave and explained who I was and that I wanted to do some training with him. As luck had it, Dave had a few clubs over in Wales not to far from me, just a quick trip, over the Severn bridge. So whenever Dave visited Wales I went over and re-acquainted myself with him.

Dave is a superb Martial Artist who unfortunately lost a great deal of his mobility due to a hip injury. I remembered him in earlier years as a fantastic kicker. Now he was unable to use these skills but he still had fast and sharp hand speed. What I also liked about Dave was on his seminars he gave me many opportunities to teach he wasn't just going to hog all the limelight. He was generous like this and I thank him for giving me the opportunity to show my stuff. He informed me that he would very soon like to give me the chance to grade for my 5th Dan. This was a great opportunity for me and I was determined as always that when the time came I would be ready!

Also at this extremely busy time for me I also encountered another person that would have massive influence on my future and that person was Geoff Thompson. I first really became aware of Geoff when I read his cult classic 'Watch my back' in its first printing. I was totally absorbed by the book and the life of Geoff.

The first time you read it you just see an extremely violent character. But if you take time to read it again you will see the underlining story of a boy bullied, who totally changed himself conquered and controlled his fears and became a better person in the long run because of this.

The book was inspirational for me and also it intrigued me when Geoff spoke about subjects like, the fence, action triggers, adrenaline switches and fear control. His philosophy of self-protection was quite radical. Not many people in the UK were approaching this topic like Geoff and I liked what I read.

In search of really valuable information on self-protection I had been reading books by top US experts, like Bradley Steiner, Marc MacYoung and Peyton Quinn.

Bradley Steiner's work was excellent and in the 80's again quite controversial. His system of self-defence called Combato was based on World War II close quarter, Ju Jutsu and Kempo. These books like "No second chance", "Subway survival" and "Below the belt, were excellent. I corresponded with Mr Steiner on a few occasions by letter and he gave me good advice on combat training and we discussed many aspects of real world Self-defence.

Geoff's work and approach was similar and to have somebody in the UK teaching these principles was great and I knew I just had to meet and train with him.

Geoff had just set up the British Combat Association with UK Martial Arts legend Peter Consterdine. The Association was designed to practice pure Self-protection and both men were embarking on a seminar tour. When I saw they were coming to Bristol I knew I would be there.

The venue was one of my old training 'homes' Whitchurch sports centre. On the day the centre was already booked for a large Karate tournament, so Geoff was relegated to the indoor bowling green for his course!

Peter couldn't be there that day but Geoff arrived with his wife Sharon, his brother in law and at that time his top student Alan Peasland and also another then up and coming Self protection instructor Dave Briggs.

The day was top class. Geoff started with his theories and experiences of violent situations then we went on to practice pre-emptive shots on the pads, power punching, knock-out technique, power kicking, line-ups and fence work. Later we drilled kick defences and ground grappling techniques before finishing with the customary ground grappling, all out against various opponents. The green baize of the bowling green wasn't the best of places for this.

I ended up with lots of skin burns and I was coughing up bits of green fluff for days after, as well as finding it in a many strange places. But the experience had been brilliant.

I kept in touch with Geoff and trained again some months later when he and Peter came back to Bristol. Also I visited Pete Miller in Backwell near Bristol when Geoff came to do a seminar and also at my old mate's Darren Richardson's dojo in Gosport. I just tried to get to do as many of the seminars so I could to learn and absorb information from the first class pioneer of Self-protection.

I joined the British Combat Association in June of 1995 and was determined to establish myself in its ranks. The BCA opened up many new doors to train with some of the best combat instructors not only in the UK but the whole of the world. I also got to meet and train with many new friends, colleagues and acquaintances. Here listed are a few of the top class people I've met. Alan Charlton of the SPA, Sambo Specialist Darren Richardson, Vale tudo champions Justin Gray and Matthew Evans, Sambo champion Vadim Kolganov, Dave Briggs self protection specialist, Maurice Teague extremely experienced Combat veteran, Jim Burns and Alan Peasland boxing coaches. There are bound to be more and I apologise if I have missed you out.

I got the opportunity to go on instructor's courses in Coventry and train with the best. Peter Consterdines Impact and power striking is totally awesome, it has to be felt to be believed. He is also an incredibly fit man who trains fanatically. His 'fit to fight' training sessions are mega and will leave you drained. Not only this, but his knowledge of self-protection, security and body guarding are second to none, he is really one of the premier experts in the world and we should be proud that he's British. Peter and Geoff have supplied some hard and truly memorable instructor's courses.

Others I have trained under are ex world champion and Olympic silver medallist Neil Adam OBE. A true gent and a fantastic judo man. I have witnessed and experienced Neil grappling on the mats against all corners up at Coventry and going through them, arm-baring them for fun. Also he demonstrated flawless Judo with British champion Wayne Lakin.

Many years ago when I was a young lad I got a chance to practice on Judo mat with the legendary Brian Jacks when he visited Bristol. Brian was an extremely powerful and top class champion but also was a true gentleman like Neil. These men and their like are what Martial Arts are all about.

I've also trained with Kris Whelan, Greco Roman and Freestyle wrestling coach. Kris is a little man but what a powerhouse, he has done wonders to put 'real wrestling' back on the map.

Jim McDonald ex featherweight boxing champ was another man I admired and enjoyed his coaching immensely along with his then heavy weight fighter Scott Welch, who recently appeared in the film 'Snatch', fighting Brad Pitt at the films climax. Jim's fight stories and marathon padwork sessions were worth their weight in gold. In recent times I have been fortunate to have former British light welterweight boxing champion, Bristol 's own Ross Hale come to train in my mixed Martial Arts classes. Ross wanted to learn grappling skills, which he is picking up extremely well, but also he is imparting his boxing knowledge on to the lads and me. A proboxer has the best hands in the Combat world without a doubt. If you get a chance to train, use the mitts and spar with one, do so. Ross is a superb boxer and a true gentleman.

Once again I trained with Krav Maga expert Eval Yanilov, also the brilliant Rick Young and re-acquainted myself with one of my old instructors Dave Turton of Goshinwai Combat.

I hadn't seen or heard of Dave from our GBASSDA days but I did know he was a member of the BCA.

I recall finishing the end of a seminar, hosted by Neil Adams doing back to back grappling. I was leaving the mat after about six continuos fights and the last one being a bit of a war with European Vale Tudo champ the brilliant Justin Gray. I was knackered and spitting out blood when I heard a broad Yorkshire accent say "Alright Kev?" I looked around and there was Dave, it was great to see him. We chatted and promised to keep in touch and do a seminar together. Dave would figure again in later years.

I am also proud to say I was invited to teach myself on an instructor's course and taught in some very good company and my Ju Jutsu was well-received that was a nice moment for me. I have enjoyed immensely my time with BCA and continue to be a member and as I mentioned earlier, Peter and Geoff have promoted me to senior instructor. In 1995 I was determined to establish myself within the BCA and in the latter five years have done just that and along the way met a list of great people.

Also in this year the great grappling explosion hit the Martial Arts world. Gracie Ju Jutsu and the ultimate fighting championships hit the scene and all this would change the way Martial arts would be practised forever.

I had read some years earlier about the Gracie's and their Brazilian Ju Jutsu. How it was a fantastic ground grappling art and how they were unbeaten in challenge matches. Also that the system was going to become massive and that Mel Gibson had learnt it for a fight scene in his then latest film "Lethal weapon". Brazilian Ju Jutsu appeared then to be the next big Martial art, and it certainly did become this along with other grappling systems.

When this all occurred my own Ju Jutsu classes began to get a number of new people joining, on the strength of watching Royce Gracie's victories in the UFC. Although my system wasn't Brazilian this didn't seem to matter as long as we had some form of grappling. This was fine with me and I wanted to make the most of this opportunity.

I sensed this whole thing was going to be huge and I wanted to be part of it. I certainly didn't want to miss the boat. Reality training and grappling were the buzzwords and I decided to expand this side of things in my classes.

For many years I had experimented with "All in sparring" and "Reality based training" but now I was determined to take it further and develop specific sessions for those who wanted to test their skills in a high pressure environment and maybe go on to compete.

Geoff had also been pushing his infamous "Animal day" sessions and these were getting good publicity and I knew I would also incorporate all this into my own training and once again over the coming years this would all develop big time and open many more doors.

I'm a great believer in seizing opportunities if they come along and not let them pass you by. Too many people sit and moan about what they could and couldn't do if only they had done such a thing or if only they got that break. The pubs are full on Friday and Saturday night with these characters.

I believe you make your own luck, nobody will hand things to you on a plate. You have to have initiative, drive, get up and go. You have to be prepared to work hard and make sacrifices but at the end of the day the rewards will been there.

In 1995 I seized a lot of opportunities and with tenacity and a will to succeed I had achieved much. Yet more was to come!

"A man's destiny knows that beyond this hill lies another and another. The journey is never complete"

Chapter 11

"Turning Professional"

At the close of 1995, I received the final push to try and make a full time living by becoming a professional Martial Arts instructor. I had nearly completed a year on my part time working arrangements and the firm was now looking for redundancies. Being part time I was obviously in the firing line. So when it came it wasn't no great surprise, but you still get a shock. Now I had lost my anchor, something to fall back on if it all went pear shaped. It felt strange saying my final goodbyes and knowing I wasn't going to turn up as usual for work the next week. The three-day week had been a good weaning period for me and although it was the end of an episode in my life I sensed new doors were opening.

I had definitely reached a crossroads in my life and I was ready for a change. My children were getting older and settled into their school. Tina had secured some part time work at the school, as she was an ex nursery nurse with teaching skills. I felt the time was now right to go for it.

I realised the Martial Arts work alone at this present time wasn't enough to keep us financially afloat, so I began to work on another idea I had been keen on for some time. I wanted to become a qualified fitness coach. I had been in and out of gyms all of my life. I had avidly followed loads of fitness regimes and weight training programmes and built up along with my Martial Arts training a good knowledge of the bodies functioning and how best to get it into shape.

My local sports centre (Horfield) where I had started a Ju Jutsu class, were looking for part time coaches but I needed some form of qualification to secure the work. So they got me on a BAWLA course. This is the British Amateur Weight Lifting Association. I completed two weekend seminars and an exam to get my leaders certificate, so that I could start teaching weight training to rank beginners.

Within a few months the gym was updated and new equipment was shipped in from an American firm. Life fitness. Also there was a wide range of cardio machines, steppers, cross trainers, treadmills and rowers.

I went on another week's course to learn all this new equipment and also the theory behind exercises, muscle working, anatomy, proper programme organising and teaching methods.

I passed these exams and acquired NVQ level Coaching certificates. I was now doing full gym induction's, personal programmes and working with and supervising schools whilst they used the facilities.

This work grew and I was employed at other Bristol city council sport centres and my schedule got busier.

Sometime later I paid to do another intense week's course with Fit to Perform Ltd. This course went into the finer points of exercise, nutrition, physiology and personal fitness programs. Once more I passed the oral and written exam and felt now I really could make a go of this side of things.

Over the years since I have worked with all types of people and advised and helped them with their fitness. From school children, the elderly, physically and mentally challenged, clients referred from the doctors with serious health problems and also sports specific groups or individuals. I have met some wonderful people, some very ill people who have shown great courage to even come to the gym and as usually as some oddball characters.

The job has given me a better understanding and tolerance of people's different levels of fitness. Because I was fit and came from a background of hard physical pursuit, I had to re-educate myself with the average person's fitness needs compared to the serious competitor or athlete It has been a great learning experience and today I am a well-established fitness coach with Bristol Community Sport a branch of the City Council.

So 1996 started with me pushing on to establish myself as a professional full-time coach shared between my two pursuits. Also I was keeping my magazine articles going and writing my books. I was building up a demanding but rewarding schedule. When people thank you for your work, your guidance or help and show genuine appreciation it makes everything worthwhile. It was something I hadn't experienced very often in my own regular eight to five jobs. You do get a great sense of fulfilment and it boosts you to try harder and reach further.

In March of this year Dave Vincent came to Bristol for a seminar and to grade me for my 5th Dan black belt. I knew again that this would undoubtedly be a challenge. But I had been meeting so many recently I was ready for anything plus I felt at my peak physically, not only in my fitness but also my technique.

I remember the seminar for one of those massive throwing marathons that Dave and Micky seemed to favour. This one was a 'throwing pyramid' where you started off throwing each other five times each with a hip throw followed by five pushups. Then move on to 10 throws and pushups, then 15, 20, 25, 30 and when you reached the top of this pyramid you started coming back down again to 5. This is a massive throwing regime, it took nearly half an hour and many people after were badly de-hydrated, physically sick or just collapsed in a heap on the floor.

I honestly gave it my all. I stayed focused, gave and received the throws and did not falter. I was on turbo boost and nothing was going to stop me that day. After the throws we went through many Goshin close-quarter combat drills, incorporating strikes, joint locks, chokes and takedowns again this was another hour.

After a lunchbreak I was taken to one side by Dave and put through a whole regime of Ju Jutsu techniques. I demonstrated 25 different throws, 25 different joint locks, 25 strangles or chokes. Defences against frontal and rear grabs, defence against punches, kicks, knives basketball bats, coshes, bottles, firearms. Then it was padwork. Standing to floor padwork. Techniques using the baton, Yawara-Bo, fighting knives and makeshift weapons. Ending with ground grappling and anatomy and physiology questions. It was a full and demanding grading but at the end I had done it, I had achieved the grade of 5th Dan. It had been a long, tiring but hugely successful day and Dave had been great, giving me every opportunity to show what I could do. Plus once more my 'lads' didn't let me down and gave a great performance.

Other avenues were also beginning to open for me teaching self-defence. I was putting my skills to use with varied groups. I taught over 50's groups, specific ladies groups, schools and most challenging wheelchair bound disabled.

I got involved in the latter project through another local council, who rang me up and asked if I could teach physically disabled anything about self-defence. I said yes and immediately took up the challenge and with the support of local authorities and police I taught a six-week course. It was hugely successful and I did a lot of thinking on my feet and adlibbing as I went along.

A lot of these people had lost the use of their legs or had multiple sclerosis but their upper body strength was really good.
I got them hitting the focus pads with palm heel strikes that carried enough impact to put the most determined of attackers on their back.

Basic self defence against holds or people blocking their chairs all went down well along with advice on security and awareness. The highlight of the course for me was getting one of the male participants out of his chair to practise simple techniques from a lying position, which he performed wonderfully. This group of people were really great, they gave everything a go and I found the whole thing hugely uplifting and rewarding. We also got coverage on local BBC television and Radio Bristol where I was interviewed. It was the first time I had been involved with the media and it was an enjoyable experience and not to be my last!

I had decided it was time to branch out and start a children's class, something I hadn't considered before. Through my coaching certifications I had learnt the correct way to coach kids and was prepared to put this theory into practise. I was to teach a very different method of Ju Jutsu, eliminating all the more dangerous and combat elements of the art. No chokes or strangles, no jointlocks (as young bones are still developing) and no dangerous strikes were some of the techniques to be excluded. Also you must remember children haven't developed the explosive short term endurance of adults so they are better suited to longer endurance type fitness but you must also never forget some will have a short concentration span, so training must be varied and constantly moving. These points and many others must be considered to run a safe and professional class. Also because of the close contact nature of Ju Jutsu you must be careful how you teach children especially the girls. Good safe and thoughtful methods will put them at ease and you will be trouble free.

I had seen some terrible teaching over the years at children's classes on my travels and I wasn't about to make the same mistakes.

My three children joined the class at various times and have all developed into good Martial Artists. Maybe one of them will follow in their Dad's footsteps. I have never pushed them to train, they have just grown up with it and took to it all naturally. It has given them all good fitness and self-confidence, which in this day and age children need. Also it has honed their discipline and respect which in modern times can be lacking in many youngsters. Martial Arts has been good for them and I am happy that they have wanted to carry on training even with the hard demands of schoolwork and the pressures it brings.

The children's class started off slowly, but then through word of mouth things began to pick up quickly.

I was learning all the time but enjoying it, as it was a totally different challenge to teaching adults.

The class now is well established with forty or more children training from the ages of six to fifteen. It has a good atmosphere. All ages mix without bullying or ego. I have some very promising youngsters who will go on to good things if they stick with it. Plus we have a nice blend of girls and boys. Also we encourage parent interest and backing which is also nice.

Over the years I have had various people help me coach the large numbers but have then moved on to other things. At previous my good friend and Ju jutsu student Dave Tanner is my ever-present co-instructor and Ross MacKenzie one of my up and coming brown belts has also just come on board to help out. I am most grateful to both for their contribution and teaching.

The children's class gave me another television opportunity in August of 96 when a children's weekend programme called 'No naked flames' asked if they could film my class, as they covered different sports or recreations each week. The programme went out on ITV.

We filmed outdoors on the grass, as the weather was glorious. The kids done brilliantly demonstrating lots of different aspects of Ju Jutsu. I done an interview and then I had to teach the young lady presenter some basic self defence moves and she then performed them on me. It was all good fun and an interesting experience.

One part I do recall was when the TV host had to perform a full shoulder throw on me as a counter to a rear choke. Now when she completed the move she had to say a short closing sentence. But each time she done it she made a mistake on the dialogue. I tell you being dumped continuously from a shoulder throw onto some sparsely grassed area was getting bloody painful to say the least. I was glad when she finally got it right! The things you do for a spot of TV coverage!

The year forged on, along with Ju Jutsu training I was regularly attending the BCA courses and bringing more and more of their principles into my art. The Sunday morning sessions at the 'Budokan' was taking off and the Impact side of our training was flourishing plus a lot of my students were progressing nicely in the full combat side of things and the reality pressure testing. These sessions were becoming quite notorious but although they were hard I constantly made sure they were run correctly and that everybody progressed and didn't just come along to battered.

I was still regularly reviewing videotapes, reading, researching and attended seminars to bring the latest and best techniques to my classes. I always felt Bristol was a little isolated from the main sources of Martial arts training but I was determined to put it on the map and kept pushing the profile. It took a lot of hard and single-minded work but a day didn't go by when I didn't take another step forward.

I had many ideas and projects but a lot fell through or didn't materialise. Sometimes you meet people who promise you wonderful things and then let you down. I have found because of this over the years I trust very few people and have built most of what I have achieved by myself with the help or guidance of a small group of trusted friends and colleagues. These people are true to their word and will not let you down. You people know who you are and many thanks.

At this stage of my career I began to feel that I could actually make a go at this full-time coaching. Up to that period I did subconsciously wonder if I could keep it all going. This is not because I didn't believe in my abilities but because I didn't know if I could get the breaks needed to further myself.

During the year of 96 I worked tirelessly to get my name around, try and get on the courses that mattered and to meet the right people that could open another door for me.

By doing this I got to be invited to teach on seminars. My good mates Darren Richardson in Gosport and Alan Charlton in London invited me to hold seminars at their dojos or national courses. I also organised a multi-styled course down here in Bristol with other local Martial Artists' joining in and training together. I had Martin Hurd of Muay Thai, John Bennett, my old Aikido instructor, Simon Evans of Taekwondo and myself teaching Ju Jutsu. It was a good way to break down barriers and get people of various arts to mix. Sometime earlier I had taught on another mixed course in Bristol which united me with Andy and Chris Davies, who I hadn't seen since my early Kung Fu and Taekwondo-days. We had all come along way since those times.

I regularly hold now a shared seminar with Martyn Hurd. Martyn is a British middleweight Muay Thai champ and a top class instructor here in the Southwest, along with his partner John Munden. We do a 'standing to floor' seminar mixing Muay Thai and Ju Jutsu together for MMA fighting. We have had good success with the idea and hope to keep them running in the future. As this year came to a close, I had completed 12 months as a professional full-time coach in Martial Arts and fitness training.

I had totally changed my life around. I had met new friends, new contacts, new colleagues and was getting satisfaction from my work. This I felt good about and I aimed to keep working to expand in the coming year.

I had begun to change also as a person. In the last few years of my employment in the timber yards, I had grown to be very aggressive and short-tempered. This really wasn't me but pressure and a dislike for the job was weighing heavy on me. Plus I was doing some hard and heavy contact training, sparring and fighting and I had began to enjoy the violent nature of the Martial Arts too much. I begin to develop a bit of a morbid fascination with darker subjects of combat. I was seeking out and reading books entitled, killer elite, Death Dealers manual, Bare kills and Black medicine, amongst many more jolly little titles became a little obsessive and dangerous to know, but I didn't realise it at the time and I don't suppose any body wanted to tell me!

At this time I did upset people and to some may not have been a very likeable person. Once I had broken the stranglehold, the job and the environment had on me it was like a new lease of life. I became more fulfilled and my aggressive nature subsided. I didn't need to use this side of me to get things done or influence people. I took a change for the better and learned to control my emotions. I wrote about this aspect of my life quite extensively in 'Bad to the Bone'.

I felt through the hard training and pressure testing I had found myself as a person and squashed a lot of my fears and bad memories of childhood confrontations or ridicule and bullying. I no longer wanted or needed to carry this aggressive approach around with me. Through changing my life and setting out on new paths I have become mentally stronger and have disciplined myself greatly in my life and taken on more than I have ever dreamt I could handle. I also begun to realise real strength come from the inside not the cosmetic show of muscle on the outside!

'Change is not made without inconvenience, even from worse to better'

Chapter 12

"My personal training methods"

Those that know me know that I pride myself on fitness and looking after myself. Since my early training days I have found ways and means of always exercising, no matter where I am.

I have found over the year's people make excuses about the fact they haven't got time to exercise, or their gym hasn't got the right equipment or they haven't got the room, space, and necessary apparatus. These are all excuses and 'kop outs', I believe you can train anywhere with next to nothing as long as you have desire, hunger and spirit. I have never let circumstances defeat me from not training. I have just rigged something up and went for it.

I can recall at fourteen years old getting my Dad to rig me up a punch bag in the garden. We didn't have much money to go out to buy the proper kind so my old man got some sand in an old polythene bag and we sewed part of an eiderdown around it. This was hung by a rope onto part of an old door frame upright, driven into the grass. I used that 'bag' relentlessly everyday when I came home from school. If it had been raining or frosty the previous night, the sand went nearly solid but I still worked away on it, in all winds and weather.

Dad also made me my first pair of wooden nunchakas which I though was brilliant and which I still have somewhere. I practised with them all the time, knocking lumps out of myself but still persevering.

At Christmas I used to get some of the latest fitness fades like the 'Bullworker', push ups bar, doorway chinning bar and that steel springy thing you bent in half (remember that?), wrist grips, wrist and ankle weights, finger strengtheners. You name it, each year I would ask for something different and then spend hours working with these things. Later as I got older I could afford my own weights, bar, and bench and used these for years in the confines of my house.

As the children were born the equipment kept getting relegated to a different part of the house and although sometimes it was a pain to set up and be quite awkward to use it didn't deter me.

When I didn't have equipment I improvised. Dips between chairs, doorway chins, calf raises on the stairs, inclined pushes ups off the steps, squats with a sandbag across my shoulders or just go out with a pair of army boots on and a loaded rucksack and run five miles up my local cycle track. I ran in baking heat, rain and gales and snow; it never stopped me it just built my spirit and resolve.

I hate running, it hurts my bad ankle and leg. Sometimes after I run I have a job to put weight on my right ankle for days. I have made myself do it and gradually increased my distances. I've run on all surfaces and done loads of sprint and hill work using many drills from Peter Consterdines 'Fit to Fight' book.

I have pushed myself to many extremes running. One regular training routine I did for a year, every week, was I ran five miles up the local cycle track. At around the 2 and a half-mile mark was a steep incline, which brought you back up onto the main road. The incline was winding and demanding. It became my nemesis each week as I would make myself run up and down it ten times before I would turn back to complete my other two and a half miles home. Each time as I neared the spot of the incline I had a feeling of complete dread through my body because I knew it was going to blow my legs and lungs away. It would have been so easy to pass it by but I wouldn't and didn't I conquered it in the end and built up enough physical and mental muscle to get up and down the slope with more to spare.

I have done this sort of thing so many times in my life. Setting another physical challenge and seeing what I could do. It was this inner battle that I have fought all my life. If I read about somebody else's training and I hadn't tried their methods I would be straight to it to test myself. Things like Ken Shamrocks 500 free squats routines, Geoff Thompsons 40x2min. rounds on the bag. Peter Consterdines hillwork and pad drills, Steve Redgraves 2000 metres rowing routines and so it goes on and on. I thrive on the challenge and won't let advancing age deter me.

I worked on my running to the stage where I have run four Bristol half marathons, covering thirteen-mile courses. For somebody who at one stage of his life had a job to walk properly and wouldn't cover any distance without moaning I am pleased with what I have achieved. To do these runs my ankle has to be strapped up like a mummy to last the pounding it will take. The last two miles are always completed on pure mental strength as my ankle by then is screaming with pain but I have never stopped or walked the course.

I like to challenge myself and throughout the years I have read and followed different people's training regimes to see how I faired with them.

I have a great appetite for new and innovative training. A lot of my knowledge was pooled to produce my 'Impact' tape series, which show many various exercises, drills and routines.

Outside of Martial Arts I have as mentioned I completed running races. I have swum in a swimathon for charity, where I completed 200 lengths of an Olympic pool. Now I don't hate swimming as much as running but I am not the world's best swimmer. I completed the whole 200 lengths in breaststroke and was in the water 2 hours 25 minutes. Obviously because your in the water you don't realise you sweat but when I got out I found I was badly dehydrated and walking on extremely rubbery legs. Also that amount of time in the water can play havoc with your bladder as it fills up. At one point it was so full I felt the weight dragging me under. I tell you peeing and swimming at the same time are an art, so to is making sure you keep your mouth shut!

I have completed in fitness challenges in gyms, 'fit to fight' nights at my classes where we would relentlessly do 2 hours of hard exercises and endurance drills. Outdoor challenges like Assault Courses and circuits.

Some years back I even done a trial for the 'Gladiators' show. I travelled to Bournemouth to go through a regime of time trials on different fitness exercises and do some 'duelling' with the pugil sticks. I unfortunately didn't make it through as the second time up a 30ft-rope climb my arms just seized and I slid back down to the bottom taking many layers of skin from my palms. I needed a bucket of water to cool them down. Fucking hell it hurt. I was desperately disappointed but what a great experience.

A few years later I did get to compete with a Gladiator Champ. One of the ladies champions was from Bristol, Janet Allen. At the local sports centre where I worked we had a 'Gladiator day' for the children. There were different events similar to the real game.

At the end I got to fight on 'Duel' with the pugil sticks against Janet. Needless to say she beat the crap out of me and knocked me off the platform. She was very good though and I was a bit off balance when she hit me! Well that's my story and I'm sticking to it!

I must admit over the years I've found it hard to turn down a challenge. I suppose that all stems back to my early school days when I felt I could have done so much more but never had the chance to prove myself.

When I was training for my fourth and fifth Dan black belts I trained everyday for months on end in my dinner hour, when I worked in the timber yard. I rigged a gym upstairs in one of the warehouses with the help of my work colleague and black belt instructor Andy Wintle. We rigged up a six foot punch bag, a ceiling to floor speed ball, chin up bar from wood, a fourteen foot rope climb, straddle jump bench, sand bags for lifting, skipping ropes and some old rusty weights.

Everyday I would do a 50-minute workout like a man possessed. I have spoke about these workouts in my other books. I trained up there under the corrugated roof in 100 degrees in the summer and sub-zero temperatures in the winter when the icicles hung from the roof and the chill winds blasted up the docks. None of this stopped me. Whatever the weather I drenched in sweat and would use a hosepipe attached to a water top at the back of the building to wash myself down. Looking back it was extreme and some times I was wasted. Once or twice a week Andy would come up and train with me we would go through pad work, boxing, kick boxing, weapon sparring, ground grappling and Vale Tudo without fail. I must congratulate Andy on his resolve in those days because I was at my vicious best and took no prisoners but he kept coming back for more.

Then on my own I would set up different circuits to punish myself. Here is an example workout. 20 minute bag work, 3 sets of 10 long arm chins, 3 times up the rope, 50 push-ups, 50 jump squats with a barbell on my back, 10 sandbags lifts, 50 squats thrust, 200 sit-ups and leg raises, 2x3 main rounds of skipping and a 10 minute round on the standing to floor ball. Usually this took about 50 minutes or so.

I did these routines religiously for nearly 2 years. I had everybody up there to spar with from the yard and the office that wanted to give it a go. I sparred with them all including one of my managers. He was a young guy, a big lad and a bit of a rugby player. I boxed him and knocked 10 bells out of him before putting him on his ass and he called it a day. How many jobs could you be in where you get to hit the manager, great!

I went through a phrase of body conditioning and seeing that I worked in a timber yard I used all the materials available to assist me in my quest. I had a bucket of wet sand for conditioning my hands (this old standby really works). I could break one-inch thick wood with my fist, edge of hands and fingertips (no mean feat). My party piece was to punch holes through doors and have lumps of chipboard 'packers' broke over my forearms, legs, stomach and back. I found this all good fun at the time!

I learnt to break blocks and bricks with my bare hands and smash lengths of wood with my shins. This used to make some of my mates watching quite nauseous. Looking back I really abused my hands and am lucky I can still move them after the pounding I gave them. I always punched bared handed on the bag and used the traditional makiwara boards until my knuckles would bleed through the effort. Body conditioning is fine if you are sensible and don't go to extremes. When I started breaking boards with my head I realised it was getting silly and stopped these extreme methods. All arts have their own body conditioning from Karate and Kung Fu to Muay Thai. Care and a good instructor is the key to safe progress.

I was fanatical at this time for training and I was really at my fittest. I was doing a lot of competitive grappling and MMA type matches and animal day like sessions. I was very aggressive and uncomprising. I hurt quite a few people and looking back some certainly didn't deserve some of the stick I gave them. But having said that it was a two-way thing and I also took what they dished out, that was the name of the game. When I left to start full-time coaching I took a leaf from Geoff Thompson's book and trained just as if I was doing an 8-hour day.

The training sessions were mammoth. I would get up and run. Go up to the Budokan, work through 20 or 30 rounds of bagwork. Run through conditioning exercises, makkiwara board toughening drills and then do three private one to one lessons with various people. Come home read, write or watch videos on Martial Arts and then in the evening teach a class. Some days would be broken up with my gym work where I always found time to get in a workout. I did this 6 days a week. At one stage I was teaching 10 classes a week Martial Arts and 4 classes in the gym and also training myself. My workload was massive. In between this I would be writing for magazine articles and my books, as well as researching new training tapes for more techniques.

On top of this I never had a car. I hadn't driven for years I just got fed up with the expense and found I could spend that money on better things. So I would pack all my kit in a big hiker rucksack and walk or catch the bus everywhere. God I was fit!

I never missed an opportunity to train if I could. No matter where I worked I found time to train or use my work as a training tool. From my days in the Timberyard working in all weather I built up a mental toughness and will to get on with things.

I can remember going in to work at 7:30 in the morning half an hour before the rest of the staff would arrive and locking myself away in an old brick building that I used as an office.

This place had no heating or lights and at 7:30am in the winter nights it was pitch black. There in the darkness I would practice my weapon training for gradings with real Nunchakas and butterfly knives. I became so good I didn't need the light and I just developed a feel for these weapons, fantastic times.

A, workmate of mine ,Fred and me for 12 months in our dinner hour practised knife throwing. Being in a timber yard we had no shortage of materials. We would use a damaged 6ft6 door and draw a life size figure on it with certain vital points shaded in. We would then spend an hour using proper throwing knives to hone our skills. I tell you we got so good we could have pinned the wings of a fly. It was frightening how accurate we became.

I learnt the original skills from Mick Upham but me and Fred took this to another level. We became obsessed with throwing knives. Not only could we throw a proper throwing knife, we could throw penknives, sheath knives and even a dinner knife. Fred's party piece was to get hold of 10 little disposable 'Stanley' type blades and bang the whole ten in unison into a target. Over arm and under arm we could make them stick, we even moved on to axes. Crazy.

I can remember getting a young work experience lad to stand against a large sack of polystyrene blocks and Fred and me fired half a dozen knives in to the polystyrene around him, we were that good or that mad. I just loved to be doing something and impressing my skills, I couldn't stand still.

Another crazy stunt I done was when we were changing a large saw blade from a circular band saw. The new one was lying on the concrete floor teeth up like the huge round jaws of a great white shark. I bet I could breakfall and roll over the entire length of the saw blade. Bearing in mind if I missed I would be ripped up pretty badly. My colleagues took the bet and I not only cleared it once, I did it twice to show it wasn't a fluke!

Another occasion I was discussing Martial Arts with a work colleague who told me if he picked up a crowbar and attempted to hit me with it my Martial Arts wouldn't be worth a light. I was very Gung Ho at the time and told him I would take him out. This developed into an argument and I told him we would resolve it. We went upstairs and I found amongst a pile of tools a crowbar. I threw it to him and I told him to get on with it. He informed me he was really going to let fly and he wasn't holding back. (Yes it had got to that stupid stage). He went for it and within a second found himself on his back, my hand around his windpipe and the crowbar safely 'disarmed'.

He was dumbstruck and we never had the conversation again! I had to treat my work as a fitness challenge to get through the days. I used to work with some young lads and I put them through hell. We would carry hundreds of doors up two flights of stairs. I would start off with two doors; then raise the challenge to three or four and so on, charging up and down the stairs. Christ did we sweat. I used to get some sadistic pleasure out of it all. I did the same with massive loads of timber. My good mate Andy Rees with me all the way, both going like trains, in all winds and weathers. Hard graft but it kept you fit.

In recent years I have tailored my training to suit my needs. At 41 years old I can't do what I did at 20 but I can and will still train hard. I am always involved in the 'Sunday morning' classes and will still spar, grapple and fight all comers and last the pace. Recovery time gets a little longer and aches and pains come and go but my constant training has meant I could still compete at the highest level in Submission Wrestling and Vale Tudo when many others had long retired.

I believe by looking after your body, being careful what you put into it and by getting enough rest between training you can be capable of many great things even in advancing years.

I have never been a 'watching' instructor. I have always been a doing instructor. I haven't gone soft through lack of training or lost my edge through body redundancy. Even on a seminar these days I will dome the white belt and get out and train with whoever is hosting that course. I am not worried about belts, status or ego my respect has been earnt by getting in there and doing it and continuing to do it.

I have put myself through some wild and crazy training over the years. I have pushed myself beyond what I thought I was capable of doing and found great new inner strength. When all physical power has been drained away, you survive on the mental side of your training. Some people may not believe I done this amount of training and worked afterwards, but I was fanatical and became a man totally obsessed with fitness, to the point of illness. There is a fine line between both and I have cruised it many times. Some never push themselves to that limit and never realise that potential. You must be careful though, there is a fine line between training hard and training excessively. The latter can make you ill and leave you badly fatigued and susceptible to injury. Plus later on in life you may suffer because of it.

I know myself some of the things I put myself through were excessive but I know if I had my time back to do it all again I would do the same, that is the type of personality I have.

In the last 18 months or so training for the Vale Tudo MMA type competition. I put myself through a personal hell. My training partners left me many evenings in a heap on the floor after pushing me to my physical and mental limits. Many a time I lay there and thought why am I doing this? Do I need this at my age? Then the next session I was back again and putting myself through it once more. When training to fight in the Ultimate Combat I worked a set routine to get myself in shape. This is what it looked like. Mon and Wed morning 30 mins sprint and hillwork on a treadmill, followed immediately by a 20 min fast row on a concept 2. Tues, Thurs and Sun 5x5 rounds on focus mitts, shield and Thai pads, plus 30mins-grappling/floor work and 15 mins conditioning exercise. 3 or 4 rounds of Vale Tudo sparring. Tuesday morning heavyweight work 60 mins and Thursday morning 30 to 40mins bagwork followed by 2 hours of sparring. This was a gruelling routine for somebody half my age. I was also teaching my classes in between these sessions. I suppose it is the nature of the beast and it will stay in your blood in one shape or form for life.

'There are no gains without pain, wisdom without adversity'

Chapter 13

'Old faces and new faces'

1997 saw the grappling arts expanding and becoming huge. Many top instructors were coming to our shores to give expert tuition. The whole scene of the Martial Arts was changing. At this period of time the complete thing was buzzing. It was exciting and I was glad to be part of it all. I wasn't going to let this band wagon go riding on by, I wanted very much to be firmly on it and heading wherever it was going!

Particular sessions designed for grappling, hard sparring and pressure testing were getting more and more popular. At the 'Budokan', Sunday mornings and Thursday nights were two noted classes and some great training was done and much blood, sweat and tears spilt. My top students and instructors would all come together at these sessions and there was no better sight for me then to see them all drilling and working out, showing great spirit, skill and technique. All those years of teaching were beginning to bear fruit.

I had found for long time students would reach blue or brown belt and then 'drop out' of class. They just couldn't seem to go that extra mile in pursuit of their black belt. For me it was incredibly disappointing and also frustrating. That was a lot of hard work down the drain and although a few had made it all the way to first Dan, I should have had more. In 1997 though a real hard core group established themselves and has gone on from there. Led by excellent black belts like Rob Cannon, Matt Sperring, Phil Davis and Paul Flett Below this I have some great up and coming people. Ross Mac Kenzie, Steve Thomas, Pete Dunn and Ismail Kadi are but a few of the lads that will go on to bigger and better things as the years go by. This is all very promising for my clubs and their future.

Back to 1997 and one of my black belts Paul Flett who originally came down to Bristol from Durham had been a good amateur boxer in his younger days. He was keen to expand his ground grappling so in exchange I got him to improve my boxing skills.

When I had first dabbled in glove work my two partners had been six feet plus and I found it extremely difficult to get past their long arms. I taught myself to 'Bob and weave' by studying videos of Joe Frazer and the young Mike Tyson fighting. I became good at this and used it to great effect in sparring.

With Paul though, I wanted to improve my long-range game and he was excellent at this. He got me to spar round after round with him at long distance using the jab, cross and lead hook. No close quarter stuff at all. I found this extremely hard going and he 'peppered' me with his great jab. But through persistence I got better. I was a Southpaw naturally but Paul made me fight orthodox and use that left hand for jab and lead hooking. I was amazed I could box this way and it gave me more options. Every week we would dome 10oz gloves and gum shields and box all out six, three-minute rounds. No quarter asked or given. This was tough and I take my hat off to any professional boxer who climbs in the ring and does a dozen rounds. The stamina and toughness of body and mind for this is extreme. So next time any of you are at home sat in the armchair slagging a boxer off, whilst watching him on TV. Take time out and think could I really do that and if you think you can give it a try. It's a whole different world when you have a real 'tear-up' to standing punching a punch-bag.

For the boxing knowledge Paul gave me, I worked on ground grappling with him and shared any new technique I had found. He became a firm training partner of mine we worked hard together. He has gone on to compete in many different grappling based tournaments and done brilliantly well. His particular field is GI grappling and he has captured Gold and Silver medals at the European Brazilian Jujutsu Championships, amongst others.

During this period I was leaning more towards "Reality" training but I did realise that everybody who came to me didn't want that extreme test. This profession was my living and I had to cater for everybody. I wasn't going to water my art down but I separated sessions so everybody could train in the aspect they wanted to and this has worked well for me.

I still was going on seminars but now I was being asked to teach on them, which was great. I taught on Peter Browne's famous BKJJU Self Defence seminar in London. I taught along side that day the great Professor David James 10th Dan in Vee Amis Jutsu who had travelled from the USA. What a charismatic and dynamic character he was, it was good to share the same mat as him. My teaching went down well and I received massive applause at the end of the day, which makes it all worthwhile.

I taught also on Alan Charlton's self-protection Association Annual seminar with other guest instructor Bob Spour of Muay Thai, that was another good day. I travelled to many traditional or sport orientated Karate clubs who wanted to learn grappling or C.Q.C. techniques and I was always well received.

In this year I also invited Shihan Brian Cheek 7th Dan down to Bristol for a seminar which good friend Neil Bartlett helped arrange. Brian is a true stalwart for Ju Jutsu in the UK. He has also travelled the world teaching and promoting his art. It was an honour to have this man come to train.

Although our Ju Jutsu is slightly different he didn't care, we had a great day's training. What I also liked about Brian was for such a high graded and famous Martial Artist he didn't take himself to seriously.

He was down to earth, shared a joke and had time for everybody young or old. I admire him for this, I have all the time in the world for this sort of person.

I have met so many instructors that are the total opposite. They are wrapped up in their own self-importance and are legends in their own mind. I have found these people to be rude, arrogant and egotist. They spend a lifetime slagging off others, their art and their methods and try to impress on you how wonderful they are.

I have no time for this. My theory is the Martial Arts world is a vast one and there is room for everybody. If we all were the same the place would be boring. If somebody sees something in a different way or teaching in a different manner than myself then fine I am not the least bit concerned.

I didn't care what an instructor is doing in their class in Glasgow, London, Manchester, and Cardiff or even up the road. That is their business let them get on with it. I afford them that respect and I hope they afford me the same.

Instructors who go around continually slagging off others are insecure of their own abilities and jealous of what others have achieved. As I said before opportunities are out there for everybody. You have got to be prepared to stop moaning and get up and grab them.

Martial Arts are the same as any other business. You are always going to have competitors, some better than you, that's life you have just got to do your best and that's all you can do.

The people I admire in Martial Arts are those who have achieved greatly but when they meet you they always ask first what you have been doing and how you are getting on.

I have met too many of the other sort who will impress upon me in the first five minutes of meeting their life history and how deadly their system is and how much better it is than anyone else's. Who are they trying to convince, themselves or me? Do I give a damn either way? Anyway back to my travels!

I was also going over to Wales on a regular basis. I had met two guys from Newport, who had come over to Bristol and trained with me privately for some time and now they had opened small classes and asked if I would go over to Newport once a month to teach and monitor their progress.

One of these guys was Ian East, a very good Judo man. Ian was a giant of a guy. Around 6 feet 4inches and 17+ stone. When I grappled with him it was like rolling with a grizzly bear! I learnt much from these sessions though and it improved my gi work no end, as he was a very competent newaza man.

The other man was the incredible John Wetter. He was in his early 60's when I met him and he was an exponent of Chinese Kempo. For his age he had incredible stamina and was as tough as old boots. His passion and desire to learn was massive and I trained him in every aspect of my combat Ju Jutsu and he could hold his own with any youngster. John's son had been a pro-boxer and had fought the likes of Terry Marsh and Nick Wiltshire amongst others in the 80's. He was a super lad and he also would come over and train with his Dad. Occasionally it would all end up with us putting the gloves on and having a spar. They were good times and I enjoyed my visits to Wales. They had a bunch of great lads over there training and they gave their all each time I visited.

Another great guy I must mention who I trained with on Geoff Thompson and Gary Spier's seminar was Judo man Aaron De Le Pledge. He was a local West Country man from Bridgwater and we had some great scraps whenever we met. He was a very strong guy with great pinning skills. I haven't seen him for years but I do remember him well.

Rupert Bancroft was another good Judo lad who trained with me for a while. He also had a wide variety of skills. He travelled around quite a bit and had trained with many top people in boxing, Muay Thai and JKD. He had also participated in one of Geoff Thompson's first 'Animal Days'. He became a good mate of mine over a period of a few years and we had some cracking grappling matches. He was considerably heavier than me and had a great Judo base but he never got the better of me! We had some marathon sessions with and without the Gi and I hope he took as much away from them as I did.

Last time I spoke to him, he had just returned from the States after a week training with Dan Inosanto, Machado Bros, Eric Paulson and Chris Hauer! What a lucky guy!

Have been lucky to meet and encounter many good people in my time as an instructor and practitioner of Martial Arts. So many that I can't possibly list them all. They're all there in the memory banks but they are just not registering at present. I have covered some ground so far, so you will know who you are if I have forgotten.

As I mentioned earlier on the grappling explosion had really hit the UK and many forms of new competition had surfaced giving particularly the Ju Jutsu based stylist a chance to test their skills. One of the forerunners was the JU Jutsu Kumite founded by Ross Iannocaro. The format was founded by the Midland based Ju Jutsu man and it has become a massive sporting competition in the UK and it also spawned the professional 'Strike and Grapple' format.

I wanted some of my lads to test their skills in this format but decided I had better try it out first and see what it was all about. Plus at 36 years old I knew my competing days were numbered!

Paul and myself entered their International Ju Jutsu Kumite Championships held in Worcester. The format was win by submission, knockout or points. Rules dictated backfist and hammerfist to the head, but no straight face shots. Kicks anywhere above the waist. Throws, takedowns, pins and submission all allowed. You were given points for different techniques, so at the end of a five-minute round if no one had won outright the leader in points would win.

I competed in the Middleweights Veteran category. I won my three fights to reach the final. The only draw back was that I had to wait nearly two hours to fight again. As you get older you don't relish this. I start thinking of being home with my feet up drinking a nice cup of tea, so I had to do my best to keep focused. I did have the distraction of cheering Paul on, who did extremely well to reach the semi-finals of the highly competitive middleweight group. He narrowly lost to three times champion at that time Trevor Cunningham. My final fight was pretty even until I caught my opponent with a backfist on the temple, which stunned him badly and almost knocked him out. Because of a bad cut he had time out to get first aid, if he didn't return after 5 minutes the bout was mine. I was only glad I didn't get disqualified for excessive contact! To his credit my opponent returned but was still groggy and I held on for the win and took first place in my category as Midlands Vets. 75 kg open champion.

I returned the following year to grab the runners up, second position losing narrowly to a man I'd beat in the championships the previous year, Steve Kilmer. I enjoyed the experience of this type of competition and brought some of my students to compete in the following months.

From these Paul and me went to Nottingham to check out the K.S.B.O. circuit run by Paul Davies and found this to also be a very good and at that time well established format. Paul Davies has worked tirelessly like Ross to bring these exciting forms of competition to the Martial Arts world and well done to them both.

Once more this year had ended on a good note and new and exciting territory had been broken.

'The only place where success comes before work is in a dictionary' *Quote.*

Me at 10 yrs with father 1971 Devon holiday

Early training in 1976

About 18yrs doing Aikido - note the hair

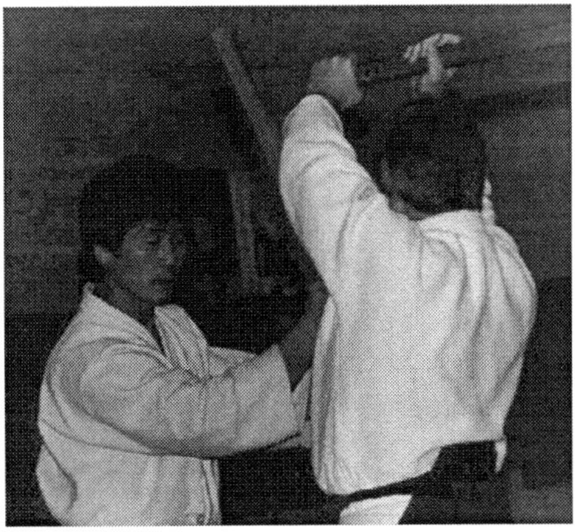

Sensei Kanetsuka – Early Aikido instructor

Training with Martin Williams one of my first Black-belts in 1984

Training with Brian Barker who helped me to establish my first club in 1982

Training in Combat Jutsu at the Old Budokan

The irrepressible Micky Upham

Pretty Boy Roy Shaw gives me a friendly handshake

My good mate and one of my first Jujutsu instructors Dave Turton

On a Seminar with the great John Macado

Pictured with Martyn Herd and Jon Mundon – Two top class Muay Thai instructors/fighters based in Bristol

My right hand man and top instructor Rob Cannon

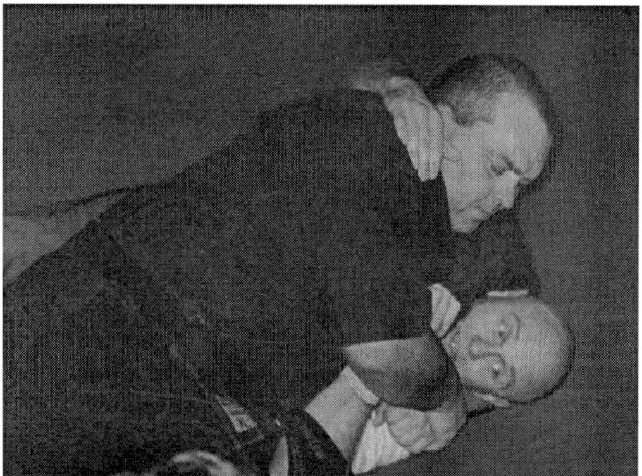

My old mate Alan Charlton of the Self Protection Association having a grapple

Sparring with Ross Hale
Former British light Welterweight boxing champion

Pictured with Ultimate Fighting Champion
'The Beast' Dan Severn

With my two top instructors
Rob Cannon and Matt Sperring

Into the mixed martial arts scene

Competing in MLSports MMA Competitions

Training hard for my Ultimate Combat fight

Fighting against the 'Combat Sports' reigning Middleweight Champion – Gareth Roberts in 2001

On a holiday break
'The old man isn't looking in bad shape at 40'

My wife and Soul-mate Tina

My children
Thomas, Lauren and Jacob

‘On the Mats’
My second home

Grappling
One of my favourites

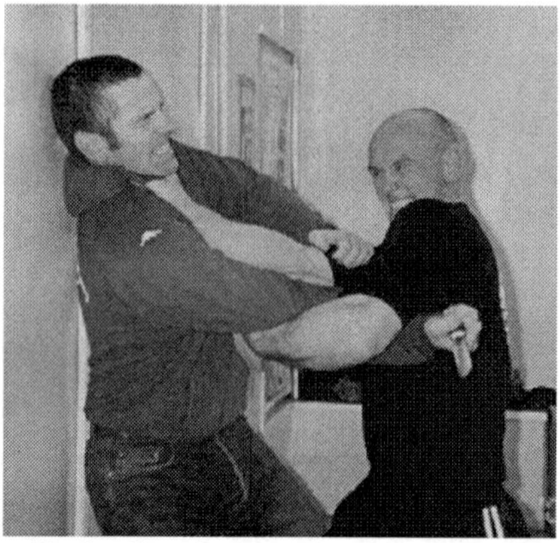

Realistic Combat and related training still a passion of mine after 30 years

Two people that I've mentioned in the book Terry O'Neil and Jamie O'Keefe

Chapter 14

‘Memorable Training

When you get the chance to train with some of the best, it really puts you on a high. Around the period of ’99, I managed to do this and have lasting memories of the occasion.

Brazilian Ju Jutsu had now settled into the UK. In Birmingham the Gracie Barra run by Maurico Gomez and in London, the Anaconda club run by Chen Morales, were both becoming established venues for this art. Maurice is the uncle of Renzo Gracie. Renzo being the cousin of UFC veteran Royce.

Renzo came to Birmingham for a weekend seminar and Paul and myself secured a place on it.

Renzo is a top class Ju Jutsu exponent but also a world rated Vale Tudo fighter. To be in this guy’s presence and have him instruct and fine tune your technique was a great moment.

All his techniques were executed very smoothly and technically with power but also grace. He was a very approachable man and spent time with everybody on the course and gave them all photo opportunities at the end.

Renzo demonstrated on one day his Vale Tudo techniques and strategies, showing takedowns, avoiding strikes and ground submissions. The next day was Gi workout. Throwing, takedowns and ground grappling were covered in good details. He also spoke at length about his training regimes, fitness and diet and passed on good advice for those wishing to compete. It was a truly excellent weekend and a memorable experience.

Sometime later I got an invite to Bob Breen’s Academy in London. Bob was hosting a seminar with John Machado. John Machado is a member of the famous Machado brothers that also includes two of the world’s greatest Gi grapplers Reagan and Jean Jacques. Machado’s are cousins of the Gracie family. John has a reputation as a master technician on the floor.

He had literally stepped off the plane from the States and come to the seminar venue, but he still put on a tremendous performance, showing little sign of jet lag.

The seminar had a select number attending and some very good ground grapplers indeed were amongst them.

The day started with entry techniques to throws and takedowns. Then ground drills from open and closed guard, then submission work.

After a break John said he needed waking up a bit and proceeded to ground grapple with a dozen or so opponents, one after the other.

This was a great part of the seminar to see his smoothness and power in action. He reminded me of a big cat playing with their litter. Sweeps, reversals, chokes and arm-bars were applied to hapless opponents. At one stage he achieved the mounted position on an opponent and whilst this lad struggled to escape frantically, John held the mount and re-adjusted his Gi top and re-tied his belt.

I took a turn to 'roll' with him and I gave it my best shot. I don't really know what percentage of effort he was working at, but I survived without being submitted although he did control the situation. I was proud and pleased to have had the opportunity to 'take to the mats' with the great man.

Later the class split down into two groups and us seniors were allowed to do some back to back grappling bouts. We did four or five each with John Machado supervising. Paul who had come with me and myself had some 'cracking' fights with some really talented and skilful opponents. I certainly knew I had been in a good workout when time was eventually called. I recall a young John Kavenavagh on the mat. John had gone on to be one of Ireland's and indeed the UK's premier MMA fighters.

To end the day we had a question and answer time with him and he candidly answered many varied questions and talked about Brazilian Ju Jutsu in his home country, the States and the UK. It was another superb training experience.

Another great seminar that sticks in my mind from that period of time was one organised by my good pal, Alan Charlton. This was one of his SPA's annual seminars and he had my good friend Dave Turton teaching his brand of Goshinwai Combat on it. It was good to hook up again with Dave and everybody gave it their all training in some brutal and painful street combat techniques.

Dave is a fountain of knowledge and wisdom on the practical side of Martial Arts and just listening to him speak is worth the asking price for the course.

But that day Alan had also captured a special guest speaker and I mean special. None other than Roy Shaw. Roy is a famous ex-bare knuckle fighter, pro-boxer, unlicensed boxer, legendary street fighter and hard-man.

Roy came to speak and promote his best selling autobiography 'Pretty boy'. This man has really seen and done it all and lived to tell the tale. He spent a large part of his life in some of the worst prisons in the UK, including a spell in Broadmoor. He has come through this dark side of life and is now a successful and respected business man. But he still has a big reputation and nobody messes with Roy Shaw.

Roy spoke openly about his life, his fighting career and some of the brutality he has faced. He spoke and demonstrated his fighting technique and took a question and answer period. Obviously he wasn't used to this sort of scene but he handled it magnificently.

My highlight was to get a copy of his book personally signed and a photograph with the man. I also got to speak personally with him and ask him about his famous encounters with Lenny 'the Guv'nor' Mc Lean. What struck me about Roy was to him fighting held no mystery. It was something he had done naturally just like eating, talking or sleeping. There was no ego or boasting about what he had achieved, it was just a part of his long and lively career. I must say on the day even in his 60's Roy looked in tremendous shape and when you looked into those piercing blue eyes you knew he was still capable of looking after himself. Another great moment in my training to remember. Roy mentioned on the day how hard we as martial artists had trained, I think he found it a little comical how we strive so hard to learn fighting techniques. This man was a natural born fighter. If you ever get an opportunity to see any tapes of his fights I highly recommend them.

At the end of 1999 I attended the end of the year instructor's course held by the B.C.A in Coventry. Geoff Thompson and Peter Consterdine were taking his one.

The course sticks in my mind particularly for a display of pure power, aggression and endurance fitness from the great Peter Consterdine. This man's level of fitness and skill has to be greatly admired. He is constantly pushing himself to new goals and I find him extremely inspirational as he is also not a man in his youth!

I witnessed him perform these '90 second' all out power punching drills on a large kick shield held by a brave partner. The idea is to punch completely all out and as hard as possible with every shot over this 90-second period until you are totally spent. Take a short 20-second break and then do 60 seconds in the same manner. Take another short break and then 30 seconds in the same manner. These drills are absolutely exhausting and have to be tried to be believed.

Peter totally punched himself to collapse. He bent the shield with awesome power and nearly bent the guy in half that was holding it. Not much in the Martial Arts world these days really makes me stand in awe but this display did!

Later he demonstrated his conditioning and mental toughness by letting Geoff who was gloved up throw punch after punch into his midsection and ribs without flinching. In the end Geoff was exhausted from punching him. A truly tremendous display.

The whole 'fit to fight' workout, which was done, was great and pushed you towards your limits and beyond. It was no wonder why this man is highly regarded in his field, he is premier class.

I have been on many seminars some good and some bad. I have become choosier on which one's I attend. I suppose after nearly thirty years in the Martial; Arts world there isn't much that's going to get you excited anymore.

We in the UK have been lucky enough in the last five years to have had some top class Martial Artists visit or shores but we shouldn't forget we have got plenty of unsung heroes here in the UK. Time to stand up and be counted guys and don't hide those lights under a bushel.

The one thing I have always done is going on a seminar to learn and bring back with me new ideas different approaches or compatible technique to add to my repertoire. I do not just go to seminars to say I have trained with so and so, or get my photograph snapped or buy the T-shirt. All nice things but you have to do something with what you have learnt.

I have trained on pre-emptive strikes with Geoff Thompson and Power strikes with Peter Consterdine, brought these drills to my club and drilled them for months to make them mine. I have attended seminars with great grapplers and come back inspired to spend longer on the floor trying to perfect the techniques. I have wasted nothing. I have notebooks from the 80's documenting techniques I have learnt on seminars and who with.

My philosophy is why spend £30.00 or £40.00 to come back to your own clubs and forget or never practise what you have learnt, yet many do. Telling everybody you have trained with Royce Gracie, Marco Ruas, Neil Adams or Eric Paulson isn't enough. It's what have you learnt and developed off these Masters?

I have gone to seminars and learnt one or two new or different things but if they were good, they were worth it. I would privately drill and drill the moves to get a good feel for them and introduce them to the class. When I perform a certain technique I can remember whom from, where and when I learnt it.

Just recently I got the opportunity to train under legendary UFC champion Dan 'the beast' Severn, who had come over to the UK to fight in Ultimate Combat IV. You just can't miss the opportunity to train with someone of his calibre particularly when it is on your own doorstep.

I was amazed at how few people had made the effort to attend the day, but it was their loss as Dan proved to be an excellent instructor as well as fighter. The power of the 'beast' was unmistakable especially his awesome takedowns and ground and pound style. A superb day!

I have been blessed with a pretty good memory and a photographic mind when it comes to Martial Arts. I can go on a course or watch a video and remember a big percentage of it. If you can't do these things, write down notes as soon as possible, while the information is fresh in your mind and then make use of it. Don't just become a seminar 'groupie' turning up at all the big seminars, showing your face and learning nothing. I can honestly say I have never travelled to a seminar to watch, what's the point, get in there and experience.

I am amazed at the amount of Martial Artists who have a bad opinion of a fellow instructor and slag them off without ever training on one of their seminars, visiting their clubs or giving themselves enough time to find out what really makes them tick. Anything I have written about or spoke about has been gleamed from first hand experience or knowledge, not here say. There is too much bad mouthing and disrespect in the Arts. Don't contribute to it.

'Success is not a destination, it's a journey, it's the direction in which you are travelling'

Chapter 15

'Sampling mixed Martial Arts competitions'

The year 2000 was a year again for new experiences and tested myself in yet another arena.

The first part of the year saw the publishing of my third book 'Grappling with reality' which was received well. Also my website that was originally put together by my good friend and personal student Mark Pietrese was up and running well. The site was very professionally done and has a wide range of topics on it. (www.BristolGoshinJutsu.com)

I am no computer demon myself but with the help of Mark and later Rob Cannon the site is on its way to being one of the very best. Rob has been a great asset on this side of things and has worked tirelessly to contribute to updating the site. I am so busy with teaching that I rarely get the time to do as much with advertisements and profile as I would like, this is where Rob has come in and done a terrific job.

You need to be able to trust somebody who won't let you down and over the years I have had many who have let me down or broke his or her promises. Rob has been a loyal and helpful friend and as well as being a first rate black belt. He is constantly thinking up new ideas and proposals and is as passionate as me to take the profile of the clubs, system and the people within it higher and higher.

He also got up and running, at a later date our first and proper monthly newsletter. This is no easy task to perform and the standards are getting better and better as the months go on.

I still at this time have kept close contact with Geoff Thompson. I continually follow his work and am constantly inspired by what he does.

Geoff did a three-part interview with me for 'Fighters' magazine at the end of the 90's and in this year I returned the favour and interviewed him for the same Martial Arts publication.

Also he sent me an original unpublished copy of his hardback best seller 'Watch my back', the complete story. He asked me if I would read it and review it again for 'Fighters' magazine. I was honoured, as Geoff obviously knew many people in the Martial Arts world and he had chosen me to do the review.

It proved he felt my opinion mattered and carried some weight; I was only too pleased to oblige. Again I'm sure as a way of thanks, in the final released book in the centre where there were many coloured photos; he included one of me and him taken together at one of his book signing in Bristol. My name was also printed under it. It was a very nice gesture and typical of this great man.

Every time Geoff has visited Bristol on his book signing tours I have attended and made sure I have brought plenty of support for him. They have been great evenings and Geoff is an extremely articulate and charismatic speaker.

I believe if you give your time to others, they will give their time to you. I have lived by this principle for sometime now and I have found it always pays in dividends. In this day and age there is too much selfishness and people only think of looking after number one. That is not the way to succeed or be successful. You may well reach the top but when you get there it will be a lonely place because you will have nobody with you!

Around August of this year a young man called Dale Adams visited my club and asked to train, he was heavily into Mixed Martial Arts and submission fighting. He told me he was working for ML Sports UK and was setting up Combat Sport trials Competition in Bath, Vale Tudo rules and would any of my guys be interested in taking part.

I hadn't formally fought in this format before in the competitive arena. I had thought since my days with Micky Upham experienced 'behind closed doors unofficial bouts'. Basically just to test yourself by mixing up the fighting ranges and trying out your techniques. Ju Jutsu never really had any formal competition so a lot of groups did their own unofficial version. Some of these could be quite intense and dangerous; looking back on some of these I must have been crazy to have a go. In those days there was no insurance or rules, scary stuff. MMA may be the new extreme sport on the block in the Millennium but slightly more hybrid versions have been around since the 70's, but more 'underground' so to speak. Many traditional Martial Artists and clubs frowned upon this type of stuff. I was fortunate (if that's the term) to meet some open minded and progressive instructors. A lot of these bouts were fought with no safety equipment or gloves. Bloody noses and black eyes were a common occurrence. Even back then I was aware of the need to train upright and floor skills and also realised how physically demanding this type of format could be. Being in good shape was essential and something I have carried with me since.

Being given the opportunity to possibly have a go in the NHB arena at this stage of my career was a dream come true. Ever since the early Ultimate fighting Championships I had become hooked on this new and exciting sport and was an avid fan of the format and the fighters. Whilst watching these UFC tournaments part of me longed to have a go but deep down I really thought I had missed the boat. Now here was a chance to give it a try and I was always up for a test!

I asked around and there was good interest, especially from the lads who had been doing my Sunday morning 'Impact' and Vale Tudo style classes. The first trials were scheduled for November, so my lads signed up and guess what, so did I! Well I thought to myself if I'm going to be training them for these competitions I might as well have a go myself and experience the format. So at 39 years of age I was back in the competing arena, at the sharp end, so to speak. We all did reasonably well in the first trials. There was some top class lads here from all over the UK. Many had been doing this type of competition for some time. The fights were hard, full contact and strikes, kicks, punches, knees and grappling were all allowed. My teams were Rob Cannon, Matt Sperring, Ross Mac Kenzie, Mark Clemmings, Steve Thomas, Phil Davis and myself.

Both my fights went the distance and both were draws; I had two good and spirited opponents. One Gareth Roberts would go on to much success in the MMA arena and we would meet again. It was a great experience for all of us who entered and we met many new friends and contacts.

The same month, Rob, Matt, Paul and I travelled to Huddersfield for the British Demonstration Team Championships. This was run through Bob Sykes of Martial Arts Illustrated magazine in conjunction with the Clash of the Titans Kick boxing event.

This again was great experience for my instructors to be in a big arena with a large crowd, with many well-known Martial Artists and personalities in that crowd. There were six teams in the demonstration competing for the Millennium sword. We had trained extremely hard for this at a time when we had also been heavily focussed on the Combat sports trials. Much training had been done and a lot of sweat lost in the pursuit of both of these things. Initially you had to put a ten-minute video together, send it to MMA magazine and wait and see if you would be picked for the finals.

Our ten-minute demo was a non-stop blitz illustrating the many facets of a Combat Ju Jutsu system. Only the four of us participated and we showed standing to floor Ju Jutsu throwing and submission, multiple unarmed self defence, pad work combined with Ju Jutsu and multiple weapon defences, all done high speed, high powered and with 100% intent to a montage of Thin Lizzy's music. We booked our place in the championships and trained every week running through the demo three or four times in a row to get it right. This was a massive cardio vascular workout. By the time the November date arrived we were raring to go.

We arrived at the venue early and watched from the balcony overlooking the arena. It gradually began to fill up and the tension began to mount as the adrenaline started to flow. We were in good company with some good demonstration teams, noticeably last year's winners, Dave O'Donnell's Elite fighting Academy from London. They were very experienced demonstration players and I felt they were the ones to beat.

We were first to come out to demonstrate. As we waited behind the scenes listening to the build up and the announcement on the PA system. I shook hands with my guys and fired them up for the last time. I saw in their eyes a mixture of fear, excitement and anticipation. Then we were on. The music kicked in and so did we and we gave maximum effort and performance. The demo was demanding enough on its own but with the crowd and the atmosphere it really hit the cardio system and we were glad when we came to the end. The following demos were entertaining but I didn't feel they touched ours; it was down to the Elite. Their demo was a blend of Martial Arts, slapstick, comedy and combat techniques, all very cleverly put together, the crowd seemed to enjoy it, but I felt we were still in with a shout.

The judges called out the results in reverse order. I don't recall who was third. We waited for the second place and the Bristol Goshin Jutsu Academy was called. Elite again took first place, we were disappointed but accepted defeat graciously. I know the lads were gutted, especially Rob who still thought we done enough to pip it.

On retrospect I suppose you have to look at what the crowd wanted. I was under the impression that you had to give an honest demonstration of your system, which we did, without all the props, slapstick and razzmatazz.

Maybe I got it wrong and people don't want to see this, they rather go for the fantasy element of the arts. Never mind, we'll be back again for another try.

I do feel as a last word on this type of event it's more of who you know and not what you know. Maybe they weren't ready for a bunch of West Country mavericks (although out of the four of us, one was a scouser, one a Geordie, me part Irish and one an English man, what a combination!) For the best part of this year MMA training and competing took priority over other things although I still managed to attend a seminar in Worcester which was one of the first in the UK for the Russian CQC style "The system". This art has some very clever and unique techniques within it and the chief instructor Vladimar Vasiliev was very good indeed.

I also went over to Wales again to teach on an annual seminar for Shihan Billy Doaks, a well-known and experienced Ju Jutsu man who has amazing power in his techniques. It's fair to say that we may not see eye to eye on Ju Jutsu and are different in our approach, but I have no animosity against Billy. He does his thing, I do mine and I personally have no problem with him. If anyone is heading for Wales and looking for Ju Jutsu instruction I will always give them Billy Doaks address. Ju Jutsu is a vast art and it can have many interpretations of how it should be trained. I have met and trained with a variety of instructors in my time and they all stressed and emphasised different things in their Ju Jutsu art. My thought on this is great! Wouldn't it be boring if we were all the same or clones of our instructor? The Martial Arts world is a big wide one, there is room for everybody. I don't care what style, system or art others are training in if they are enjoying it brilliant, carry on. To clear up my thoughts on Ju Jutsu, I would like here to reprint an article I had published in MAI some years ago to sum up my thoughts on the subject.

Cross training has taken the Martial Arts by storm. Nearly everybody, unless they have been on planet Mars for the last six or seven years, now realises the importance of having a balanced fighting system, allowing you to be competent at all fighting ranges, i.e. kicking, punching, upright grappling and floor grappling. Many hybrid systems have evolved catering for this and it seems Martial Arts are heading in this direction.

I have trained in Martial Arts for some twenty-eight years now and have at one time or another experienced most arts and still actively train in any system or with anybody who I feel has something worthwhile to offer. For all this my base system has been Ju Jutsu since 1984.

When I first got introduced into Ju Jutsu it seemed a much more complete Martial Art than any other I had experienced. It also dealt with certain attacks and techniques, which I sought the answers to.

This art is probably one of the oldest in existence and has admirably stood the test of time. From being a warrior art for the Samurai on the battlefields and being taught to World War one and two soldiers, to being taught to many of the security forces of the world, to Gracie Ju Jutsu today, which has faired so well in the 'no holds barred' arena. Ju Jutsu has been a hybrid art and since its birth, it can be adapted with the times to incorporate short stances, boxing like foot and handwork, rapid fire strikes and very close quarter joint breaks, strangles, sweeps and throws. Also, it includes pre-emptive strikes and takedowns to combat the enemy of today. Impact training on pads, bags, shields, etc, are essential as is grappling and glove sparring for realism.

Although many Ju Jutsu systems still take a traditional approach to training, all have stressed an all-round knowledge of standing and floor arts for a very long time. If you look at classic CQB texts like Fairbairn's 'Get Tough', Applegate's 'Kill or be Killed' and 'Cold Steel' by Styers, all base their training around Ju Jutsu-like systems. Even today forces like the Royal Marines still use Ju Jutsu techniques as their unarmed training.

My personal feeling are that most grappling and multi-faceted arts owe something to Ju Jutsu at one time or the other.

Ju Jutsu today is a strong self defence art that is now making its name in the sporting arena, through various associations set up solely for this purpose. I recently experienced this first hand in the National Ju Jutsu Kumite Open Championships, Brazilian Ju Jutsu Championships and Amateur and Pro Vale Tudo bouts. It was a good and interesting experience. For many years Ju Jutsu practitioners had to either enter Judo or Karate competitions if they wished to compete, but of course this limited their overall effectiveness, as they like to strike and also grapple. Now with the explosion of free fight formats they can do this.

Cross training may be a new concept to some, but for the Ju Jutsu practitioner it has always been a part of their repertoire. The chameleon of the Martial Arts can adapt to anything.

In closing, is Ju Jutsu the best system to train in over other Martial Arts? The answer is NO! All arts have their strengths and weaknesses and at the end of the day it's the man in the art, not the art in the man. But if you want a good form of all round training with a good pedigree, Ju Jutsu could be the art for you.

'It takes a brave man to step out of his comfort zone and seek pastures new'

Chapter 16

'Evolving and climbing'

February 2001 saw the competing team; me included going back to the second combat sports trial in Bath. Again we made a good showing, against some even better class of opponents than the first time around.

My fight was against Paul Jenkins from Wales. Paul has a pedigree of contact fighting, from boxing, knockdown karate and Thai boxing to strike and grapple events and MMA.

To say the fight was tough would be an understatement. Paul is a big puncher and kicker and my conditioning and experience kept me in the fight. We did have what could be called a bit of a 'tear up' and it went the allotted distance and finished a draw. (At the time of publishing Paul will probably be British middleweight champion).Paul Is excellent fighter and an asset to the MMA scene.

I damaged my hand in that fight and although part of me wanted to fight again, my whole living relies on me being fit and well and able to function effectively, so I withdrew my fight card for the day.

The hand injury was on the base of the thumb and it originates from twisting that thumb in a Gi Collar some twelve months earlier, grappling. It can be fine for a while and then it will suddenly flare up if caught wrong. It is something that has become re-occurring.

A month or so later I received official notice that on my trial results I had captured a place in the national championships at middleweight. Also two of my students Ross Mac Kenzie and Mark Clemmings had also gained places in the same middleweight group. Unfortunately only one member from a club can compete in the same weight category.

It thought this over and realised that at thirty-nine years old this would probably be my last chance to compete at this level, so I asked Ross and Mark if they would step down and allow me the chance to enter. They agreed, and as both were young men, I knew their chance would come again.

The Nationals were set for June and this date would be two weeks short of my fortieth birthday, I knew I had a task ahead of me, but as always I was ready to give it a shot!

I trained hard for six weeks in preparation for this championship.

My schedule was tough fitting it around my normal teaching. I was at this stage teaching eight Martial Arts classes a week and five gym classes. My training consisted of the following on top of this. Monday: Cardio workout out in gym 1 hour or run, Tuesday: light weighted workout morning, evening time bag work, padwork and grappling training. Wednesday: heavy weight workout. Thursday: bagwork, Vale Tudo work. Friday: run. Saturday: Day off. Sunday: Impact or Vale Tudo training.

This schedule is tough enough for a guy half my age, I can tell you I was sore and had to mentally lift myself to keep the routine going. My training partners pushed me to my physical and mental limits and got that bit extra out of me.

Before I knew I had a place in the Nationals I had signed up to fight in a submission-wrestling tournament also arranged by ML sports and Dale Adams. This was to take place in May and in retrospect I should have pulled out of this event and kept focused on the Vale Tudo. But I decided to enter and have a few bouts.

When it came to the weighing I had a shock. I had been training hard on my stamina and I was down in weight to 75kg. This was lightweight and not at the Middleweight category that I was due to fight in at the Nationals. I was a little worried. It mentally threw me out. I competed in the Submission Wrestling at lightweight but my mind wasn't right.

My first fight I dominated against a very flexible and rubbery opponent who I managed to keep subdued with my scarfhold but couldn't get the finish. In my second bout against a good up and coming lad Roger Woodward. I got careless when trying to choke him out with his own belt. He slipped into a very neat armbar and I was forced to tap out. I didn't want to risk injury with the Nationals so close so I decided to submit. Taking nothing away from Roger it was a clever move but I wasn't really firing on all cylinders that day. Roger will go on to bigger and better things, he is a great young talent.

After that tournament I was concerned about making the middleweight bracket, so I had to change my training. I cut back on the cardio work and started lifting heavy weights. Basis lifts, strict and slow and at the same time I started eating for England.

Over the six week period, I touched no fatty food or alcohol whatsoever and disciplined myself to a strict and healthy eating routine. Some of it was darn right boring and repetitive, but I stuck religiously to it. On the day of the fight about a month since I weighed in at 75kg. I tipped the scales at 81kg. I was at my heaviest and I felt strong and solid.

The Nationals was a great day. A good crowd was there and plenty of support. There were championship belts and trophies for all that participated and Dale ran a very professional tournament.

I was drawn to fight Richard Stapgate. Another excellent young fighter from Wales with good MMA and NHB experience. From the trials I knew he was a very hard leg kicker and I had to get my game plan right to survive this one. It was a four-man tournament at Middleweight and no disrespect to the other lads involved but I felt I had drawn the best guy there.

The fight proved every bit as hard as I expected. Richard got some big hard kicks in earlier on and I knew I had to close the gap to survive. I did this and took the fight to the floor. Richard is no slouch there either and we had a tough battle up to the end of round one.

Round two I was fairing a bit better, my timing was getting better as I warmed up and the 'old body' begun to respond. At one stage I drove my opponent across the area with a flurry of punches, then got a headlock on him and jumped up to the guard bringing him down with me.

I felt comfortable in the guard and punches and attempted submissions were working. Richard attempted a 'bar choke' but I felt okay and defended this with no problem. Then he very quickly altered his position and slapped on a 'fig 8' choke. At first I felt no danger and then very quickly as he leant his weight in I felt the blood rushing in my ears and I knew I was on my way to 'Sleepsville'. I tapped the mat but it felt like slow motion then it was lights out.

I come around to the voice of Rob my corner man and Paul who assisted him asking if I was all right. Yes, I seemed fine after the briefest of sleeps. I was helped to my feet and shook hands with the waiting Richard Stopgate. It was all over for me but I had given it my best shot.

I had felt after reviewing the fight my opponent just had that extra edge in speed, which comes with youth, and I was just a second behind him in doing what I wanted. You can't stop the sands of time trickling away and I suppose time proved it on this occasion.

After this busy schedule, I was glad of a break and was looking forward to a holiday, which I felt was well earned. I enjoyed the break and had a change to re-charge the batteries. I find these days unless I actually get away for a break I end up falling into the trap of working in some shape or form everyday.

When you work for yourself you always end up picking up the ringing phone and doing some business or ending up arranging a private lesson, or get involved in some project. This is great and I love what an unexpected call may bring in the shape of a new opportunity but this is infuriating to the family who wants some quality time together. I have learnt with experience when to work and when to take a break from it. You need to do this from time to time so you can unwind and take things a bit easier. I treasure quality time with my family and I will not miss out on this when the opportunity arises. Anybody who works for themselves know that their business doesn't revolve around a nine to five time schedule. You find sometimes work will eat into your free time and you have to be careful to find a balance.

I try to keep and even balance and allotted time schedule for my training, teaching, clerical work, writing and research, otherwise they all overlap and you find some days you get swamped under.

When I returned from holiday, the combat trials were starting again at the end of August. One of my top students Ross Mac Kenzie was going to compete in the lightweight division so I started helping him with his training. As the training progressed I began to get an itch to compete again. I think the summer weather had eased away any aches and pains and I was feeling good, so I decided to send my entry and give it another shot.

I remember the day of the event was very warm indeed and it was extremely hot in the competition area. I was first up to fight again at middleweight against a veteran kickboxer Mark Woodall. Mark had many years of experience in the kickboxing field and had travelled extremely in the UK and around the world competing and coaching. Mark had some great fighters in his 'Roughhouse' stable, notably MMA competitor Paul Sutherland.

Mark and me were speaking before the event and he commented that he thought he would end up fighting against me. We had a laugh about this. When I was called out to fight who should my opponent be but Mark.

Although he wasn't greatly experienced in the MMA competition, I knew he was a wily opponent with first class kickboxing skills, so I had decided from the off that I would grapple him.

After an initial exchange of kicks and punches I secured a front guillotine choke on Mark. As I worked it, I jumped up to bring him down in my guard but he held his balance and didn't fall. I put my feet back on the ground, manoeuvred around a bit and put it on again but much more tightly.

I arched my back and squeezed and I felt my opponents breath labour and then he was tapping out. It had been a quick victory and I was glad of that. Mark told me after it was the tightest choke he had felt and I feel his lack of grappling experience prevented him from attempting to counter. Much respect to him. He is a first class Martial Artist.

My second bout was against a young fighter from Weston Super Mare Ju Jutsu club run by another old friend Ian Rossiter. This lad was a good amateur boxer and come out firing on all cylinders with punches. I covered, closed and dropped a good left hook to his body and took him over with a body drop throw. I fell into scarfhold position and settled it. I had managed to work two of my favourite techniques the left hook to the body and the scarfhold. I have won many matches with these techniques.

Once I settled the scarfhold in, I hooked his arm with my leg into an elbow lock and then cranked up his neck and got an instant submission. Another quick win and a good one. I was well pleased with the performance.

I had one more fight on the day in a 'freeweight' but against heavyweight Charles Halliwell from Bob Sykes Huddersfield gym! This lad had come down to fight but there was no heavyweight fighters signed up on the day, so I agreed to have a go.

He came up with some big bombs, kicks, punches and knees. Again I decided to take him down. On my first double leg attempt I got caught with a big knee strike squarely in the chest, which did knock some of the steam out of me. I went in again though and this time he sprawled back and got me in a guillotine choke. I went to sit through to counter this but in a blank moment went the wrong way, the choke became a powerful neck crank and I was forced to tap out whilst my head was still intact on my shoulders!

It had been another good day and although I had decided to enter these trials at the last minute they had worked out to be the best yet for me.

The next trials were at the end of September and I decided to enter once more as I could see a possible opportunity of once again reaching the Nationals, which a few months previously I hadn't envisaged possible.

Matt and Ross two of my top students also went again to fight in the heavyweight and lightweight division.

Once more at this event the standard was even higher than before and many competitors didn't even get a chance to fight as so many had entered.

I fought against a guy called Suley Mahmoud a pro Vale Tudo fighter from the London Shootfighters gym. It was a fast and explosive affair straight from the off but that's the only way I can go. I was looking for another quick victory.

This fight again was quite even. I felt stronger standing up this time whilst my opponent wanted to go to the floor. The fight ended a hard fought draw and both of us had felt the pace.

Again in this bout my hand had flared up, which was becoming a problem, so I decided to withdraw my fight cord to prevent further injury. I knew I had done enough to make the championships.

Matt and Ross both turned in good performances to also book themselves places in the Nationals. So for the second year running the Bristol Goshin Jutsu combat academy was represented.

Between these championships I was ranked as number one middleweight in the combat sports ratings, which I was proud of at the age of forty. Before the finals I had two seminars to teach on, both promised to be good days.

The first was for my old friend Dave Turton at his newly formed association 'The Self-defence federation'. This federation again was dedicated to the more combat orientated arts and street applied technique.

Their annual major seminar was held in Batley Yorkshire at Neil Hall's 'Fighting chance' academy. Many top named Martial Artists in the combat field attended that day and I taught combat Ju Jutsu techniques for self-defence which went down very well.

A couple of weeks later I was in Dudley in the West Midlands to teach a Vale Tudo, MMA seminar for Grappling styles international. An organisation set up by Paul Dunne through Combat Sport Worldwide for the practice and promotion of MMA and NHB competition. I am proud to be a senior instructor within this newly formed group, which is a database and forum rather than a specific rigorous and hard-training session and all that attended gave it a hundred percent effort.

I enjoy the seminar scene and this side of my teaching. It's nice to meet up with people that know you through your writing or videos who have travelled to train under you. On seminars you can meet many new friends and contacts.

I have done many varied types of seminars in the last few years from street self-defence, Combat Ju Jutsu to MMA. Also I have taught C.Q.C. for the reserve Parachute regiment organised by an ex-student John Banfield.

I have taught on numerous occasions for TA and army reserve and I have always been well received and also enjoyed experiencing what some of these guys have got to offer in the world of real combat.

I also have branched out into the field of teaching protection in the work place for corporate companies. These seminars are in their early stages, but I have enjoyed them immensely. It is a change not to have to wear a Gi and get on the mats to teach. These people want to know how to cope with violence in the work place and coping with aggression in their daily employment. I have found this sort of seminar highly rewarding as most of the participants before attending had little or no knowledge of reading the signs of danger and how to avoid it. It is a field that I certainly would like to delve further into and develop more. I know I won't be on the mats forever, so it is an outlet for my knowledge and skill. But don't worry the old man isn't quite ready for retirement yet! Safe and sound management UK is the name of the company.

The end of 2001 was the National Championships once more in Bath. Combat sports again organised a first rate event and I was glad to be part of it.

The fight card had an impressive line up and I drew to fight the reigning Middleweight Champion Gareth Roberts. We had met before and had drawn our fight. I must admit I fancied my chances of pulling off a victory.

Ross, fighting in the highly competitive lightweight division, fought a cracking fight but was caught in a triangle headlock in the dying seconds. Matt once again made it through to the heavyweight final to fight his old nemesis and reigning champion Nick Jones. The fight was a thriller going the complete distance and an overtime period with no submissions. Nick took the judges decision but Matt had pushed him all the way and I was proud of his performance.

Matt has transformed himself over the years from a quiet and shy young lad, who lacked self-belief into a monster of a man on the mats and is destined to take that title. It is a great story of courage and dedication on his part and I am glad that I have guided and coached him along the way.

As for me, my bout with Gareth Roberts was a close call. We had matched each other move for move and their had been nothing in it. Close to the end of the first round, Gareth received a 'yellow card' for an illegal move, which instantly put him behind on the judge's card.

As the second round wore on I sensed his frustration, as he couldn't get a position or submission for me.

Gareth is a leglock specialist and in the dying seconds he tried to submit me with an Achilles lock but I blocked it and stopped the submission. He was moaning to the referee in desperation, as I just had to hold on to win the match. But he showed he was a true champion by suddenly pulling a spinning knee-bar out of nowhere and I just couldn't fight it as I felt my knee straining to snapping point, I had to tap literally seconds from the end of the fight.

I was disappointed, Gareth elated, it had been a very close call, but I couldn't have done anymore. When the knee bar is set in, you can't do much about it if you want to walk the next day.

So a very busy and interesting year come to a close and I had pushed myself to levels that I hadn't realised were attainable.

'There is little you can learn from doing nothing'

Chapter 17

'Muscling In'

In late 1999 I was approached by one of my students and friend Mike Hockett and asked if I would like a small part in an up and coming 'fly on the wall' documentary called 'Muscle'. The six part BBC 1 programme was planning to follow a firm of Door Security staff for a six month period to see how they operated in the clubs and pubs around Bristol.

Mike was one of these Doormen and had trained with me on and off for a number of years. The programme would cover how they trained for fitness and fighting skills and this is where I came in.

I was only too glad to get another opportunity to showcase my skills on television. This time it would be National TV and peak time viewing. It couldn't do me no harm and hopefully send some business my way.

The BBC camera crew filmed my bit with Mike at the old Bristol Budokan, which at that stage was still open. We went through an hour of filming. We done padwork, weapon disarming, locks, restrains, pressure points, strangles, defence against holds and grabs, pre-emptive strikes and combat ground grappling.

I think the producer and camera crew was suitably stunned when we had finished. I don't think they had any idea what to expect and I turned it on for the camera, which you have to do to sell yourself and they loved it.

Because the programme was going out after the 'watershed' we could be a bit more explicit with dialogue and techniques, it was great fun. Although I don't know if Mike agreed, he was on the end of a hell of a lot of technique.

Sadly when the programme went out a lot of my stuff had been cut or edited down into just a few brief moments. But having said that it was well put together and hopefully had the right impact on the viewer.

It is amazing, the power of television. Just from those brief clips I had phone calls of congratulations and praise from colleagues in the Martial Arts world and also calls of interest about my art and classes. So it was worth while experience.

I must admit I do harbour an ambition to do some serious stuff for TV or film. I love the whole package of filming and being in front of the camera. I feel happy and natural there! So if there's any film directors or producers out there, just give me a call now, while I still have a bit of life left in me!

People have asked me about my involvement with the lads who featured in Muscle, so for the record. Mike Hockett as explained was a Ju Jutsu blue belt in my clubs and I had known for some years. I met Chris Nott on numerous occasions and he trained with me a few times. As for Ronnie Butler and security leisure boss Martin Jones. I had both heard of both but do not personally know them. My only involvement with the programme was the basic bit of filming for episode one.

Initially the programme came in for a lot of stick, primarily because of the way a situation was handled at the end of the first episode. This was when a mass fight broke out over what seemed a pretty innocuous opening scenario. The lads were slaughtered for it from many quarters. I think in hindsight they even felt they got it wrong but they can't change the situation now. In my opinion, I feel it was handled incorrectly but in their defence you can only react to how you perceive the situation in that instant. We all get things wrong in our own job on occasions, fortunately we haven't got a camera crew breathing down our necks and the outcome of our mistakes won't result in a 'kick in'. We can't be right all the time.

It was unfortunate that the whole thing was filmed for everybody and their dog to give an opinion on. I think as the series went on, it managed to give a more balanced view of the job and the guys come out of it all in a good light.

You must remember you are always going to be open for criticism as soon as you do something like the 'Muscle' programme. Also the public must remember it is meant to also have a degree of entertainment value for you to watch. Controversy always gathers viewers, it is good TV, you shouldn't take it all to heart.

From the point of view of the job of Door Supervisor, as it is known these days the majority do a great job. They see that the average man and woman can enjoy a safe night out without any hassle or trouble.

I have trained door staff and had many come to train in my classes and they have all been smashing people and not what you may expect. As I have often told their critics, somebody has to do the job.

The police haven't got the resources or manpower so these people put themselves on the line week in week out. I have experienced some work earlier on in my life but it's something I wouldn't want to do now, unless I had no other option for financial support.

You get good and bad in every line of work, door work is no different. You also have different scales of experience and expertise. Some people have vast experience and are true 'pros', top of their tree and are extremely good at what they do and nine times out of ten will diffuse any situation without the need for violence. I have been fortunate over the years to call some of these people my friends. Obviously you get some 'young bucks' go on the door to prove themselves or because they are in love with the glamorous image. Also they do it to pull pretty girls. These are all the wrong reasons and a recipe for disaster. If you land a job in a student wine bar, the likely hood of serious trouble kicking off is pretty slim and you can get complacent and think you are a top dog. Work in the city centre in a large night club or pub venue and it can be a totally different ball game, you need to be switched on at all times and have 360% vision. You can face some potentially life-threatening situations and you have got to ask yourself do you want all this? Some can stand the heat others can't, my advice to anybody thinking of going into the door security world think hard about the reasons why you want to do it.

When it comes down to physical skills I would say the majority of doormen are average or below average fighters. I am talking from the viewpoint of a professional Martial Artist. I have trained lads that have Great Spirit and heart but not particularly good fighting skills. There are other door staff that are already skilled fighters and have brought that expertise into their work. There again are many young lads working the doors who believe they are bullet proof and they may be in for a shock when the real deal shows up and wants to kick off. A few months Muay Thai, Karate or Wrestling isn't going to stand you in stead for the reality of a brutal street attack.

For most part a doorman's job will involve tact, diplomacy and good conversational skills but when it gets down to the crunch you need to be able to efficiently look after yourself. Many are all front, buff and talk with very little else, the cream is in their minority. As mentioned in some of my previous books having a shaven head, tattoos and every orifice pierced doesn't make you a hard man nor does heaving a few weights about. Some believe this is enough.

These are superficial barriers put up to warn people off and they may work well, until a professional sees through them, looking the part isn't the same as being the part. Luckily the average punter doesn't know the different but there is always one who will and they will take you right up to the doorway of violence to find out. You have got to be prepared for this moment and be trained appropriately. Many aren't.

Some are living on reputation or past glories. As I stated earlier as you get older, there is always some young gun looking for a scalp, make sure it isn't yours!

Door life is a hard life, you don't get much thanks for it and inevitably you can't win, one minute you are a good guy, then you are a bad guy. A crowd in a pub or club can be a fickle lot. A group of lads can come in a club all smiles and greetings and come out baying for your blood with hate in their eyes. In this day and age with more and more drugs on the streets and mega strong alcohol people can be dangerous and unpredictable.

For those of you who watched 'Muscle' you witnessed this for yourself, I think Martin Jones and the other lads did a good job over all. It's easy for somebody sat in the comfort of their armchair to give their opinion but it's not the same as being out there doing it.

I take my hat off to the 'pros' that do and do it well, the night-club culture is a safer place with you guys in it. Respect.

'Door security are a bit like police, everybody hates them until they need their help'

Chapter 18

'Training in your forties'

I am often asked how I have kept a high standard of fitness as I have got older. There is no secret to this; it takes a lot of hard work and dedication.

From my point of view I have always trained and have never had a long break or period of time away form it. So if over the years the hard base of fitness and conditioning has been built, it is down to me to maintain and preserve it.

Obviously at forty years old you can't do what you could at twenty, (we are talking training here, guys). You have to adapt, so that you train smarter and not harder.

Your body obviously takes a lot of punishment over a period of time, particularly the joints. They get natural wear and tear anyway, but with constant punching, kicking and joint locking they will take tremendous strain. I have to discipline myself to a certain way of life if I want to still be at the top in my field, this requires a vast amount of self-denial and self-control.

When you are in your youth, you can go out on a Saturday night, sink seven or eight beers, go clubbing, have a takeaway and tumble into bed in the early hours and then get up and train the next day, no problem. You can also train everyday with no after effects and go balls out all the time. Now I can't do this all the time. I still train hard but I pace myself and train at different intensities.

As a professional instructor and trainer I train or coach most days. I will have days where I will work at about 60 – 70% of my maximum, whether it be in the gym or on the mats, nothing too intense, just a nice light workout but still keeping up my base level of fitness and conditioning. Three times a week I will go for a harder workout, pushing up the pressure to maximum working on my anaerobic fitness and explosiveness. This can be done with bag or padwork, sparring or running, rowing, stair climbing or cross ski trainers in the gym.

To maintain my strength I have one really heavy weight session a week. I will work on strict and big compound exercises like squat, bench press, leg press, clean and press, dead lifts etc. I find with my other training this is enough to maintain my strength.

I don't lift like a body builder, which I made the mistake of doing in my early days. I lift for functional muscle strength for my Martial Arts. I will maybe get another weight session in but this will be working to about 55 – 70% of my capacity concentrating on muscular endurance and explosiveness have also developed a special workout with a weight plate, outlined in my video impact jujutsu vol.3.

Every class I take I will still front the warm ups, which will consist of stretching, plyometrics and callisthenics (Hindu squats, Chinese push-u, 'V' sit-ups, neck bridging, mountain climbers, burpees, star jumps etc). This again keeps up my endurance, strength and functional muscle and burns body fat.

In heavy workouts include my Sunday morning classes which I still participate in. These are geared for Vale Tudo and reality fighting and I will spar, grapple and workout with my fellow instructors and students and still push them to their limits. The next day though I will take it more steady to allow my body to recover and ease muscle soreness.

As you get older, recovery time becomes longer between workouts, so you must get adequate rest, good food consumption and get in the right vitamin supplements. Food is your bodies' fuel; if you put crap in your system you will get crap performance. I eat very little sweets and chocolate and consume a small amount of alcohol. I can relax with a bottle of beer or a glass of wine and leave it at that. I can take or leave alcohol and I am not governed by it, as some are. I keep down the intake of fatty food, so if I have chips or a 'fry up' it is a treat rather than a weekly occurrence.

I get plenty of complex carbohydrates for fuelled energy, especially before training and get good sources of protein after for re building the bodies tissue. Eating certain foods at the right times can help body recovery and replenish energy quickly.

I believe my eating habits have kept me in shape and maintained my fitness as much as my training. But it takes will power to resist or walk away from food you like.

Most people's concern about eating certain foods is becoming fat and gaining weight. Although I am wary of this my main concern is being healthy on the inside so my body is functioning correctly and can perform when required. It is a big and important subject (hey there might be a book in it!) that would go into many chapters to explain fully.

I feel the old saying 'everything in moderation', still holds true in most cases.

Vitamin supplements I have also taken for years and will take a regular batch every day and occasionally try others. The regulars are multi vitamins and minerals, vitamin C, Zinc or Selenium, Odourless garlic, chondroitin and Glucosamine and desiccated liver, amongst others. What are their functions?

Desiccated liver to transport oxygen in the red blood cells.

Glucosamine and Chondroitin to ease joint soreness.

Selenium to cleanse the body of damaging free radicals

Garlic for a healthy heart

Vitamin C to help fight infections or germs (colds)

Multivitamins to supplement anything I may miss in my diet

Co Q 10 a sparkplug for energy

Ginko Bilboba Improve reaction of the brain

Omega 3 and 6 for essential oily fats for cholesterol levels and healthy heart

Some people will say supplements are a waste of money, but in this fast paced work place, if you don't always get the opportunity to eat properly supplements can help. Whey proteins mixed with Amino Acids and Creatine can also be great sources of fuel for building muscle and endurance. But get some expert advice before taking and make sure you have no allergies to these things.

There have been many debates over the supplement Creatine. Does it really improve your strength or fitness capabilities? Can it damage your liver and have other side effects? Well I can only give you my own personal view on this subject.

I have taken Creatine for some years now and I feel that it has definitely improved my strength levels in the gym and my performance on the mats. I have taken many different so called 'miracle' supplements over the years but Creatine is the only one I can say that has given me positive results. The only side effects I have experienced are the occasional upset stomach. But in general if you stick to the proper guidelines I feel Creatine can enhance you fitness performance. I will usually go on it for a month to six weeks then come off it again for the same period of time and then start again. I have found this the best way to use the supplement. If asked does Creatine work? My answer would definitely be, yes, but you have also got to put the effort and work in whilst you train to gain the benefits.

Stretching is getting more and more important in my training. I have never been a massive fanatic of stretching but I have disciplined myself to do more and more. Flexibility in the neck, back and hips are essential for grappling and I feel a good stretching routine reduces a lot of muscle stiffness and soreness for me.

I read years back in the footballer Tony Adams Autobiography that he reckoned that when foreign coaches and players come into our game, they brought the importance of pre and post stretching and this extended his career by years. I have to agree on this fact, if your muscles are properly stretched the likelihood of strains or pulls are greatly reduced as you advance in years.

Rest is also important; if you train hard you must find time for adequate sleep. Staying up late all the time leaves you lethargic and listless the next day and then you struggle to train. Again footballer Stuart Pearce who is still playing at top level at 40 years of age gets eight hours sleep every night without fail.

All these things I fully believe keep me going. As I said there is no magic formula but there are guide lines and you have to have a lot of will power. Look at a man like Helio Gracie now in his 80's but will still get on the mat for a 'roll' with his sons. This is all due to proper care and attention to his body. I hope I can do this with my children when I'M that age! The bottom line is you can't abuse your body and get away with it, in the end the effects will catch up with you and it will breakdown. Look at what happened to the football legend George Best, who in my opinion was the best footballer on the planet. He never reached his full potential and threw this talent away.

It amazes me how people can utterly abuse their bodies and let's face it when it ceases to function so do you.

Apart from my training, I want to be fit and healthy enough to enjoy my life. Do things with my family, go places and travel. I don't want my health or lack of it preventing me from doing these things.

When you're young you take fitness and health for granted. You take getting up out of bed as norm, as you get older you realise it is a precious gift and one we have to look after.

I am proud of my fitness. I am proud I can still workout and compete with lads half my age, but I know I can't take any of this for granted and I have to work sensibly to do this.

I have done some crazy training over the years, mega sessions that have taken me to the brink and beyond. Not all of them good for me and I have now become more educated in when to train and when to rest. When you get this balance and you can stay injury free, there is no reason why you can't go on training for as long as you wish. I feel too much emphasis is put on age in the Western world, where's in the Eastern climate people go on achieving amazing things to a ripe old age. It's all down to an attitude of mind.

Tell somebody often enough they are past it and they will begin to believe you and act accordingly. Redgrave didn't listen and went on to win a fifth gold medal at forty, Holyfield didn't listen and regained the heavyweight championship at thirty nine, as did George Foreman at forty two. Footballer Stuart Pearce won't listen to you about age barriers and neither will Helio Gracie. You can be the same.

I know however old you get you do not lose the 'fighters' mentality. Once a fighter always a fighter, although you may cover up that secret. If you have lived the life of a fit, strong Martial Artist it is very hard to relinquish that title. I fear the day I don't feel capable of looking after myself and I pray it doesn't come but you realise you can't fight old father time, he is the one opponent that will beat you in the end. I just want to keep the bastard at arms length for as long as possible! That's why I am not ready to give up the fight just yet and I won't be adverse to still doing some crazy things. It's what keeps you alive, so that you don't lose your edge or spirit. I sincerely believe if you still want to compete at high levels your first goal is to stay fit and conditioned, you must have pride in yourself and look after your body.

So for all you veterans out there, train smart and keep heart and you can still cut it when needed.

'A lot of people have gone further than they thought they could because someone else thought they could!'

Chapter 19

'The Ultimate Martial Art'

What is the ultimate Martial Art? This question has been put to me on many occasions and it's been one I pondered myself in my early Martial Arts career.

My answer to this question now is quite simple. It's not the art in the man but the man in the art. There is no one art that has all the answers. Some come close but don't make it all the way. Every art has something to offer and can be adapted to work in a real situation.

Some will say Shotokan Karate is not a particularly practical are. Tell that to Sensei Terry O'Neil who has spent a lifetime in the art and adapted it for working on the 'doors' and for street combat. Indeed the late and great 'daddy' of practical and realistic street fighting Gary Spiers was a traditional Karate man.

These men and many like looked beyond the traditional aspects of their arts and made it work, they were also not afraid to step outside of their art and experience other fighting systems.

Aikido has been knocked as an impractical art but I can show you individuals who can adapt and make their technique work in the real world. You see these individuals didn't run with the pack, they broke away to experience and experiment so they had a practical and powerful fighting system.

Indeed all the great Masters and founders of the major Martial Arts systems were innovators and people, who looked to improve, modify and develop their arts.

Is Boxing better than Judo? Karate better than Wrestling? Muay Thai better than Ju Jutsu? How can we determine this, they are all different and effective in their own way. If one Boxer beats one Judo man can that be conclusive evidence of its dominance?

In the early days of the UFC, Brazilian Ju Jutsu was being hailed as the ultimate Martial Art. But three or four years down the line Brazilian fighters were being beaten by kick boxers and wrestlers. Did this mean Brazilian Ju Jutsu was no longer effective? Of course not, it is down to fighters not styles. There are good and bad in every art.

At the top of the tree most Martial Artists will agree, you need knowledge of more than one art to be a rounded fighter.

I honestly believe at hand range a pro-boxer is king, their speed, power, reflexes and movements are awesome. But if a boxer is on the floor, the grapplers become the masters. It's a proven fact and most of us know that by now. The UFC, NHB and MMA scene has gone a long way to hammering home this fact.

So if there is no ultimate art is there an ultimate fighter on this planet? Sometimes we hear of the heavyweight boxing world champion as the best fighter on the planet. In the realms of the boxing ring, yes he is, but what about in the Octagon of mixed Martial Arts or on the pavement arena? Men like Frank Shamrock, Tito Ortiz and Rickson Gracie have been called complete fighters. But this is referring to the arena they train in, not as a whole. The street arena for instance is a world apart from any sporting competition, no matter how few rules are involved.

I know men who may not fair too well in the ring or octagon but have literally stared death in the face and won. Men who have worked and fought on the streets all over the world in the capacity of security, bodyguards, forces or police. They have defeated attackers armed with knives, bats, axes, firearms and more. They have survived mass and multiple attacks and fought in dozens and dozens of real world scenarios. Are they the ultimate warriors? See it gets hard when you broaden your field of vision. Read Kate Krays books 'hard bastards' 1 and 2 then decide if the guys in those pages are bad, mad or just sad. Are they ultimate warriors?

I feel it's down to a specific person for a specific job. For example a Ferrari is a fantastic example of a fast and powerful car, it's up at the top of it's league, but if I was going to do some off the road driving it would not be on my list of effective vehicles. See what I mean its horses for courses.

Over my years of training I have made truly wonderful exponents of their given arts. Neil Adams, powerful and superbly executed throws, Kenpo Master Larry Tatums awesome hand speed, John Machados's effortless ground grappling, Peter Consterdines one shot KO power and so on and so on. All have dedicated a lifetime to their chosen pursuit but all would readily admit as good as they are they are not masters of every range of combat, although they may have working knowledge.

I personally believe there are not enough hours in a lifetime to be an ultimate fighter, but you can certainly gain a working knowledge of all ranges for your own self-protection.

I do think though you should have a base art to work from and then build upon it.

Ju Jutsu has been my base art since the early 80's but over a long period of time I have added other skills from different arts to my system. This didn't happen over night. When I wanted to improve my ground grappling I spent hour upon hour for 18 months to begin to get to a good standard but I am no where the best. When I wanted to improve my hand technique 6 months solid every week I was in front of the heavy bag and floor to ceiling bag, sometimes 5 times a week, punching and punching. I could box eventually three to five rounds full out amateur level but I wouldn't have lasted long at pro standard, these guys are a different breed.

You see a lifetime is not enough to master everything. Not if you are honest with yourself and get your head out the clouds. I have seen people punching a heavy bag or the pads and believe they are boxers. Reality check. Get in the ring with a 'real' boxer and you will see the difference.

You may spend years perfecting boxing skills but what about kicking, then we have throwing, let's not forget ground grappling. See what I mean, not enough hours.

Look at Manchester United, without question over the last I don't know how many seasons they were the best football team in England. But would those players be also the best cricketers or rugby players after 6 months training? Of course not. It's a different ball game altogether, you have to view Martial Arts the same.

I have devoted a large chunk of my life to the Arts and I honestly will say to you under extreme pressure of real combat I am a moderate kicker, a reasonable thrower, a good puncher and a competent ground grappler but not a master of any range. That's me being honest. To up the percentage on the different ranges I have good conditioning and a tough mind set and fighting spirit. I believe the ultimate fighter has not been born yet. Will there be such a person? I don't think so, but it certainly is fun debating and discussing the subject.

Finally what we must be aware of, there are people out there that really do believe they are the ultimate warriors, beware of these characters. They believe their own type and visualise themselves as the new Bruce Lee.

The Martial Arts world is full of some weird, wacky and eccentric people, as well as would be Ninja Turtles and Power Rangers!

I pray to God nobody views me in that light.

If anybody out there does I will have to tear out your heart with my secret iron claw killer Shaolin technique or tap you on the nose with my delayed death touch, so at least you'll have time to finish this book before you die in terrible, screaming agony, ha! Ha! 'Nuff said!'

'No ultimate Art, Just Ultimate fighters'

Chapter 20

'The weird and wonderful'

Through my years of training I have experienced some weird and wonderful things as well as many humorous moments. In this chapter I will touch on just a handful of these things to show what a mad and unpredictable world a Martial Artist's can be at times.

I have been lucky in the fact that I have received very few serious injuries whilst training and touch wood neither have any of my students. I do remember on one occasion when one of my students came over to me and said that he thought he had 'done something' to his finger. I asked to look at it and sure enough he had. His middle finger was dislocated at the first joint, so that the top of his digit was facing skywards whilst the rest of the finger was horizontal. I told him I could put it back in for him but it may be a bit painful. He agreed for me to do it. I told him to look away, grabbed the finger and pulled sharply on the joint and in it popped! He was fine and pleased as punch; off he went to train again. I was happy all had gone well.

Five minutes later he was back to me showing me the same finger pointing again skywards. He had caught it once more and dislocated it. I repeated the process and put it back. This time I taped his finger to the next one and advised him it was probably best to leave the training for the rest of the night. I laughed to myself of the likelihood of the same accident happening twice in such a small space of time.

I must hasten to add here putting back dislocations are not medically recommended and can be unpleasant for both participants. But sometimes as an instructor you have to think on your feet and improvise.

On another occasion I had a lady join my class who told me she had had a car accident a year previously and as a result of her injuries her shoulder had a habit of 'popping out' of joint. Somewhere in the back of my mind I mentally made a note of this fact and as it turned out it was just as well.

Halfway through the session I noticed her on her hands and knees cradling her shoulder with a concerned training partner looking over her. As I approached the training partner said that they hadn't done anything and that the lady had just done a basic backward breakfall and now this had happened.

I could see the lady was in some distress and pain. She told me that the shoulder was dislocated and pleaded with me to put it back in. Now fingers I have done a few times, shoulders that is different. I said it was probably better to call for an ambulance and get a professional to look at it, but she was in tears and begged me to give it a go. So with a silent prayer and some basic idea, I held her arm at the elbow and elevated it up quickly. "Click". The shoulder was back in. She was smiling, I was relieved and the class thought I was a hero. Result!

I am glad of my constant first aid training and highly recommend every instructor to be trained in it, as you never know when it might come in handy.

In my capacity as a fitness instructor, I take clients in the gym for induction to learn about the equipment.

Usually I do these in the mornings and some people may not have had breakfast before coming along (not the right move) and consequently whilst standing up and watching my demonstrations they get light headed.

A few months back as I was sitting on a hamstring curl machine explaining to a group of about half a dozen people, a lady near the back just suddenly fainted and ungamely slid down the wall to a seated position, luckily she hadn't keeled over headfirst.

By the time I reached her she suddenly came round and was more embarrassed than anything else. She didn't have any idea that she had fainted. It was so spontaneous.

On another occasion as I supervised a group of fifteen or sixteen year old school kids, a girl just fell off an exercise bike, where she had fainted whilst cycling.

Again fortunately she wasn't hurt but a bit confused and extremely embarrassed. A lot of young girls at this age skip lunch or eat very little, so any type of vigorous exercise is going to affect their blood sugar levels causing them to faint.

I must admit I became a bit paranoid of standing groups on the induction for a while as I expected another to keel over at anytime.

As mentioned earlier I also work with people referred for exercise by their GP's. You really have to pay close attention to them as some have very bad heart problems, blood pressure, or asthma amongst other things. Again you do get a little paranoid waiting for every gasp, sigh or sudden movement. It really is an experience.

I have witnessed also some funny sights although at the time you have got to be professional and deal with it.

People falling of treadmills and rowing machines can be a hilarious sight and you often wish if you had a camcorder at hand you would make a fortune on "You've been framed".

I have been asked many strange, crazy and provocative things in the gym and dealt with all manner of people.

On one occasion I was working out myself when a lady approached me who I had seen in the gym on many occasions. We spoke and she told me she was a physiotherapist at a local hospital and she was teaching students in their last years of training. She asked if I would like to go along to a class and be a model, so that they could make a real life study of the muscles they had been learning about. Being the shy and retiring type I immediately said 'yes'

So a few weeks later there I am stripped to the waist with about twenty young ladies viewing my body from different angles and asking questions. I know it's a dirty job but someone's got to do it, I got paid for two twenty-minute classes as well. Can't be bad. That certainly was an odd request.

On the subject of modelling again my physique got me onto another little job. I was on holiday in Menorca with my family and we took a coach trip to the capital Mahon. The trip included one of these free trips to a fashion show promoting leather goods. (No whips or masks were included).

A group of us sat either side of a catwalk sipping a free glass of champagne whilst three attractive lady models got ready to show a variety of leather coats.

The lady organising the event came out and explained her male model hadn't shown up and would anybody like to volunteer. My hand shot up and I could audible here groans from my wife and kids. Dads about to make a fool of himself again. In I went to the back with the other models and was shown a very nice leather jacket, which I would have, to parade in. I was asked my name and waited for my call.

Once I was called, out I came and strided off down the catwalk and turned around and came back. Seeing it was a so hot that day and I obviously didn't expect to be modelling, I had just worn a vest top and shorts, some how the leather jacket on top didn't look that classy. Still I received a generous round of applauses and I took overzealous bow before leaving.

The kids were mortified after my return but Tina just gave me that look that said I've seen it all before!!!

Martial arts have also brought some strange and funny moments.

I have taught all over the place from large sport centre venues to outdoors in the woods, in an Indian restaurant, my living room, garage, Private girls school, school fêtes, village fares, scout clubs, TA centres, office blocks, prefab huts, prison, schools for behavioural problems, disabled centres, army bases o on and so. All in the name of Martial Arts.

I've trained myself, everywhere and anywhere. There is never an excuse not to train. I have fashioned and made training equipment out of any material to help me improve my skills. I believe if you want to train you will train anywhere, no excuses.

Wherever I worked in the past I found somewhere to get some training in even if it was only for twenty minutes or half an hour.

When I wanted to learn the nunchakas and the Filipino butterfly knife I would get into work half an hour early, go to a quiet or empty part of the building and practice. I did this day after day until I began to get a feel for the weapon. I was lucky that I worked in Timber Yards so I could find a deserted spot. I trained in the pitch dark of an early winter's morning or when it was so cold my hands were frozen. I forgot the amount of times I lumped myself with the nunchakas or cut my fingers with the balison knife but I would carry on working at it. I must have looked a right madman if anybody had been watching me!

As mentioned earlier on when Andy and me trained in our dinner hours we used to go at it full out. Many a time we were rolling on the floor exchanging punches or attempting a choke or armbar when a member of the public had came across us. There would be a look of disbelief and shock on their faces as they walked off. Many a customer in the Timber Yard had remarked to the other staff about some lunatics training upstairs!

Martial Arts demonstrations were always fun moments, where you have to expect the unexpected. Things never pan out the way you plan and you suddenly have to adapt and change tactics at the last minute.

I did a demonstration once at Leyhill Open Prison. One of my black belts Mike Griffin was a PTI there and got us a spot at their annual fair. It was a beautiful summer's day and three of us decided it would be perfect to train on the grass, no mats needed. We were all prepared and ready to go when half an hour before our time a shower of rain came down. Now this made the grass top very greasy and slippery.

Our footing wasn't as sure as it should have been and I can tell you when we got to defending against weapons (knives, bats, chains, etc) we had to be spot on as you couldn't afford to slip otherwise you were in danger off running onto one of those things.

Another time I did a demo for my kids school fete. Again it was a very hot June Saturday. My guys and I put down some PVC gym mats on the grass a little while before the demonstration time. Unknown to us the sun was beating directly down on the mats and was nearly melting the PVC. We were training in bare feet and after we had made the introduction and then stepped onto the mats, it was like walking on hot coals! We started off throwing each other around and it was a blessed release to land on your back to get your feet off the floor. We ended up disregarding the mats and having to do the rest of the demo on the grass. I can tell you the soles of my feet were blistered after that afternoon. You live and learn!

On another occasion back in my Aikido days, the clubs did a demo at another fete in Dursley, Gloucester. We done the demo in a roped off area with a good crowd watching. In the background here the Red Cross first aid people idly watching and chatting. The close of the demo was myself and my instructor demonstrate knife defences, using a real but blunted knife. Up to this point the Red Cross had been pretty disinterested but when they saw this rather large knife flashing about, they were over and gathered right by the roped area and waiting intently incase one of us made a fatal mistake. Luckily we didn't but I think it ruined their day as they were on the starters block with bandages at the ready!

Again in my Aikido days, me and a good mate Mark went to do a demo to open a new club. The instructor was Mike Narey, a well known face in the Aikido world. Mike basically bounced Mark and me around showing the more dynamic techniques of Aikido. Whilst doing this he accidentally elbowed Mark on the nose, no problem we all kept going. We stopped and Mark and myself had to face the class and go through some cuts with the bokken (wooden sword). As we started, Mark's nose began to drip blood. First slowly, then as he increased the speed of his sword cutting technique it got faster. Now Mark was one of those guys that just kept going unless he was told to stop. Mike was behind both of us so he couldn't see what was happening. The assembled crowd watched, eyes getting wider by the moment as a crimson fountain was spilling down Mark's white Gi. I desperately tried to catch Mike's attention to. Eventually he spotted it and told Mark to stop and clean himself up. I'm only glad he saw Mark when he did otherwise I had visions of his whole Gi turning red and the whole crowd passing out!

As you can guess from earlier in the book my old instructor Mick Upham was an unpredictable force. Once on a large multi styled seminar, one high graded instructor whose name I don't recall was teaching on one of the mat areas when suddenly he was called to the phone. Before leaving the mat, he looked around and spied Mick and asked him if he would take over whilst he was gone. Mick comes on, takes centre stage infront of all these eager people ready to train and says 'Right then, do you want to carry on with this shite or shall we get real?' The assembled group was gobsmacked. I had to stifle a laugh. Mick was a premier ball buster and didn't care what people thought of him. Many didn't like his methods but would not tell him to his face.

The late great Gary Spiers also was a man who took no prisoners on his seminars. Once on a seminar in Bristol, he spied a couple of young student lads not taking the training too seriously. He targeted in on one of these lads and said, 'What's that written on your forehead?' The lad was confused, 'What do you mean?' He asked. Spiers replied,' Do you know what I can see on your forehead?' The kid shook his head. 'I 'll tell you son, fucking victim, that's what I see! It ain't your fault lad but if you don't do something to remove it you are gong to run into a whole lot of trouble.' The lad was dumb struck and Gary patted him on the back and walked off. Priceless.

You never know what to expect from people that join your classes. Most are great but the minority can be strange. I remember in my early teaching career, I brought a class to an end and whilst we knelt down, I asked them if they had any questions they wished to ask. Obviously in relation to their training. One elderly guy put up his hand and said, 'I have a problem, Kevin' 'Oh yes, what is it?' I asked expectedly. 'Well it's my cockatoo!'
I was momentary thrown, 'Sorry' I replied. 'Well whenever I practise my moves at home it goes wild in it's cage and makes a hell of a fuss.'
By now the rest of the class were pissing themselves with laughter, but this guy I could see was deadly serious. Trying to control my own laughter I said in my most serious of voices, 'Maybe you should put a blanket over the cage so he can't see you.' He thought for a moment and then quite seriously replied. 'Yes I think I will do that, thanks!'

Fights? I had more on the mats than ever off them. As a young man in his twenties I relished at any opportunity to test my skills. On any seminar I went to I always seemed to encounter somebody who wanted to mix it and I was only happy to oblige.

I wouldn't let anybody take liberties with me and if they did they were in for some fun. A few moments stick out in my mind, although at the time they were far from humorous.

Again in my Aikido days I was training at my club with a guy called Mervin. He wore a hearing aid and everybody always made allowances for his lack of hearing and I felt he played upon this. We were doing Jo techniques (4ft wooden staff), one for one. After a few goes Mervin brought the Jo crashing down on my head and it bloody hurt! He mumbled he was sorry so I let it go. A few minutes later he did it again. Was it lack of control or was he just trying it on? I told him this time to control it and be careful. Low and behold a couple of seconds back into drilling he done it one more. This time I was angry and felt the anger rise inside me. Did I notice a glimmer of a smile on his lips? I took a deep breath. My head was throbbing with three distinct lumps rising on it. I was not a happy man. These Jo staff were made from solid Japanese red oak and that was bloody heavy. I waited for my turn; deflected Mervin's Jo and brought mind down with considerable force squarely on his skull. Take that you fucker I thought to myself. He went down like a pack of cards, stunned, in a heap. Unfortunately my instructor was passing and saw me do it and I was admonished for dangerous practice. Still it was worth it. Needless to say I didn't have any trouble from Mervin again!

I had so many similar incidents over the years; I forget more than I remember. I know that I went through a proving stage and seemed to always be in conflict. For me Martial Arts training was a serious business, I didn't do it in any half measures and I expected others to be like minded, of course this wasn't always the case and I am sure over the years people thought I was too hard or severe with my training.

I recall once again in my Aikido days as an Orange belt when this guy joined the club who had come from America. He was also an Orange belt and had gone to great lengths to tell me how he had been training with Chiba Sensei and other top Japanese. My initial thoughts were great, another good person to train with. The first time I paired off with him I realised he could talk the talk but not do the walk! After I had thrown him over two or three times in my usual style, he started telling me how he had a back problem and could I go easy. Then he was using stalling tactics by doing up his belt or fixing his Gi. This all served to infuriate me as I felt he was a fraud to his grade and couldn't have worked as hard as me to earn it. After this and on every possible occasion I tried to partner him and give him some stick.

For all his shortcomings he was still training and trying to bullshit us with name-dropping and tales of his training. In the end he would do his utmost to avoid me and would skirt around me as I approached him to train. One night after training we were all having a drink and he opened up and admitted when he came to our club it had frightened him. He said he hadn't trained nowhere near as intensely as we did and he had struggled badly. He turned to me and said I had literally given him nightmares and he had avoided me like the plague. I admired at least his honestly and we shook hands and I agreed to help him out. From then on we got on all right, but some months later he returned to the USA. About six months after this I heard he had received his Dan grade, which was incredible. Luckily he never came back to train at our Dojo, otherwise I would have helped him out via the window!

I have met so many people like the above man, who are in love with the idea of training in Martial Arts but are living in a fantasy realm, visualising themselves as some great warrior or fighter.

I mentioned earlier about going on a seminar in Ninjutsu, where senior instructors were impressing upon all who were present about how they wanted their art to be taken seriously and that they didn't want to be seen as comic book figures hiding in the dark and performing exotic tricks and techniques.

Then in the lunch break I watched two guys clad in black from head to toe trying to 'capture' each other with weighted nets and swords. There seemed to be some sort of paradox going on here.

Sometimes whilst teaching things don't always go according to plan and you just have to improvise and go with the flow. On one occasion I was teaching on a seminar and I called one of my lads out to throw a punch at me so I could demonstrate a certain counter. This lad had a terrific and very awkward right hook, which caused a lot of us problems.

I was flowing, on a high and getting good response from the gathered group. I asked him to throw the punch, but I wasn't concentrating fully and the hook went around my cover up my guard and connected hard with my jaw. Luckily for me it was high up on the jaw and not on the chin. It connected with a sickening dull thud and I felt the blow. I shook it off and said 'See how difficult it is to block a punch, you can't afford to let that happen.' I then just carried on showing it correctly. The group must have thought that was one hell of a graphic way to get your point over!

At another seminar I called out a young lady who used to train with me called Rachael.

She was a tough girl and would mix it with any of the men and hold her own. Some time though she could be full on and not pull her punches. At this course I brought her up to show how a lady can defend herself if grabbed from the front. I wanted the scenario to look as real as possible so I steamed in and grabbed her hard and forcefully in a bear hug around the waist.

Her adrenaline must have kicked in and without an ounce of control she head butted me in the face, sunk her teeth into my shoulder (bloody hard) and kneed me in the testicles. The watching group was stunned but not as much as me! I could easily have gone to my knees from the groin shot but gritted my teeth and working to my full professional capacity I turned to the group and just said 'See, that's how it's done!' (Spoken in a rather squeaky voice!)

I always enjoyed demanding training and one of my black belts that I mentioned earlier Mike Griffin was always up for this and we had some wars together. One of the things we would do regularly at the end of a class would be to attack each other randomly, one for one with grabs, holds, punches, kicks or weapons, standing or on the ground. It usually started off pretty sensibly and then deteriorated into each of us trying to come up with a worse and more awkward type of attack. One evening we had pretty much exhausted our repertoire and Mike had me pinned up against a wall in a frontal body hold, crushing the air out of my lungs. He was grinning and saying 'Come on then, how are you going to get out of this?' I waited to the moment was right and then clamped my hands firmly to his face and kissed him long and hard on the mouth! I tell you he dropped me faster than hot coals and was gagging and spitting and rubbing his mouth whilst he was doing this, I shot a kick to his groin and a following elbow to the spine (I pulled these) and retorted "that's' how." He was never the same again!

As mentioned elsewhere our rituals for fooling about knew no bounds. My all time classic came when I was invited to Mike's 'wedding do' on the evening after he had got married. Mike had hired a nice hotel and all his family, relatives, work colleagues and friends were there. I arrived with a few others from my club and mingled in and had a drink. I asked where Mike was and I was told he was up on the dance floor doing karaoke. He had had a few to drink and was doing his George Michael impression (no, he didn't have his trousers down!).

Now Mike wasn't a drinker but hey it was his big day so he was celebrating. I hunted him down and he had drawn quite a crowd with his singing.

There he was still in morning dress giving it stick. He hadn't noticed me so I crept up behind him and grabbed him by the balls! I lifted him and took him to the floor. Mike was to say the least taken by surprise! The assembled family and friends were in shock thinking 'Who is this bald maniac attacking Mike?' I loved every minute and caught him good and proper. We laughed about it later but at the time I don't think he found it too funny.

At this time Mike had been pestering me about grading for his second Dan and I kept telling him he wasn't ready, but at every opportunity he kept on and on. So I thought up another little 'surprise' for him on his wedding day.

At the night party there was a table laden with wedding gifts which Mike and his wife would open when they returned from their honeymoon. This all gave me the idea. I wrapped up in special wedding paper a brand new white belt and labelled the present, 'to Mike from Kevin, something I knew you've been waiting for'. I put this amongst the other gifts. Now I knew Mike was desperate for his second Dan and I also knew when he read the label he would think his grade had arrived. Can you imagine his face when he frenziedly tore off the wrapping paper to find a white belt! I just wish I could have been a fly on the wall at that moment. He gave me some stick when he later caught up with me, but it was worth it!

Sometimes I feel you can get obsessed with training. When I was really going through a mad stage of ground grappling I found it started to overlap into other areas of my life. On one occasion as I was walking along the road and an old boy in front of me dropped his walking stick, as he bent down to pick it up, I came from behind, put my 'hooks' in and flattened him out for a rear stranglehold!

On another occasion I was having a moment of romantic passion with my wife I even started to pass the guard!! I tell you that was bad enough but the finishing armbar really pissed her off!! These are all only jokes folks honest!

Having a lighter side to Martial Arts and not taking yourself too seriously is a must in my book. Some instructors out there are so self absorbed in their own importance they are living on another planet. I like to share a joke on the mat whilst I'm teaching. It breaks the ice with strangers and puts them at ease. Barking and growling all the time like a drill instructor from the film full metal jacket isn't going to cut it.

Another very funny incident, which happened recently, was at a Cage Fight Event. In the changing rooms of the fighters you get complimentary drinks, fruit and chocolate.

I was in there with Paul Jenkins whom I mentioned earlier on as a top class MMA fighter. He is also a joker. Half an hour before the event, all the fighters were called out individually to enter the cage and take a bow to the assembled crowd. Just as Paul was getting ready to go out he grabbed a banana from a fruit bowl and shoved it down the front of his Vale Tudo shorts. Linford Christie would have been put to shame!

Then he merrily ran out into the cage and took his bows and applause, we were all absolutely cracking up. What a stunt! I did make sure he ate the banana after and never slipped it back into the bowl. This was priceless humour and one we can all learn from (incidentally Paul went out and soundly whipped his opponent, so he didn't lose his focus).

War Stories? My God, there are so many books on the market with one person trying to out do others in the 'I'm harder than you' department. I'm not about to join the bandwagon.

I have read so many books on tough guys that in the end the people in them all sound the same. Different name, different face but same story, it all gets rather boring and repetitious. I do hope we don't get to the stage where Kate Kray is writing hard bastards 53, I don't think I could take it!

Hard? Tough? We all have different ways of interpreting the words. I spoke about this at great length in 'Bad to the Bone'.

At the end of the day every city in every country has somebody ready to make a claim or tell a story. Every man involved in Martial Arts, fighting, contact sports wants to believe they are the best, the toughest but it's all down to on the day and a bit of lady luck with you. Anybody can be beaten by fair means or foul and when you live by the sword you will die by the sword unless you can get away from that life style. I don't tend to listen too much to all these stories true or not I'm not personally bothered. I don't want to have to have a street-fight with anybody for the rest of my days.

I believe if somebody is pushed to the 'backs to the wall' limit they will fight back no matter if they are good at it or not. I would only fight for survival not for ego. Just because you don't want to fight doesn't mean you can't. At this stage in my life I have more important matters to address and different paths to explore. As you get older you don't have anything left to prove to yourself and being involved nearly three decades in the fighting arts mean you have learnt to discipline yourself and leave your aggression on the mats.

If you walk around snarling at everyone with your knuckles dragging the floor you will only have a limited number of 'friends' and options in your life.
I will say on a personal level that I have had more fights on the mats than off. I have always been lucky to be able to use de-escalation techniques and avoidance before ever having to resort to physical on the streets and I am pleased with my track record. As a man of forty plus, a husband and a Dad I don't wish to be rolling around on the pavement with some nutcase.

Hard training and adversity has moulded my character to which I have become today. Martial Arts have been my vehicle to find myself and to change my mindset and build up my mental strength as well as physical abilities. I went into Martial Arts to learn how to fight but I transcended that and found a whole lot more but for all that I have never lost sight that the Martial Arts are exactly that, fighting arts and they should be practised in that fashion.

Most people that are promoting the fact that they are teaching practical self-defence are not and that's the bottom line. I honestly believe there are only a small minority of people in the UK that really understand self-protection and are teaching it correctly. Those that have read my other books or magazine articles will understand what I am talking about, so I'm not going to expand upon this too much. I also try and keep up with what is happening in the States and in by and large Martial Artists over there have also mis-understood the concept of real self-defence. I'm not questioning their ability or techniques I'm questioning sometimes the naivety of some instructors when it comes to the concepts and scenarios of so called reality situations. If you don't want to take my word for it, please if you haven't already read Geoff Thompson, Peter Consterdine, Jamie O'Keefe, Alan Charlton, Dave Turton, Dave Briggs. None claim to be the worlds greatest Martial Artists but they are the main men when it comes to the harsh realities of real world self-protection.

Traditional Martial Arts is not self protection training it is Martial Arts full stop. Kickboxing, Point Karate, Semi contact fighting and sparring is not self-protection. Even the exciting and often brutal sport of Mixed Martial Arts and No Holds Barred training is not self-protection. Let me expand upon this is the next chapter.

'The best self defence technique is not to be there when trouble kicks off'

Chapter 21

The face of reality

November 21st 1993 changed the face of martial arts world forever. It was the date of the first Ultimate Fighting Championships. This show, and many that followed, had a significant influence on the way martial arts would be practised in the future. Firstly it woke the sleeping giant called 'grappling'. Brazilian Ju Jutsu was the forerunner, followed later by wrestling. But as these matches continued we saw another change. Once the striker began to learn grappling skills he started to look for ways to counter them and make good his punches and kicks.

When this was achieved the birth of 'the cross trainer' and mixed martial artist was born and it has just grown from there.

These contests exposed the techniques that did not hold up under combat conditions. The fancy moves, the killer death touch and all the other martial art myths and fantasy were blown out of the water!

No doubt for those looking to test their all round skills in a limited rules and pressured environment the MMA Contest is the ultimate sporting challenge. It will expose your strengths and weaknesses, test physical conditioning and your mental strength and fighting spirit.

As fighting sports go it is one of the most exciting and toughest, up there with Muay Thai, another incredibly tough sport.

My clubs and myself have participated in MMA Contests in Vale Tudo, Ju Jutsu Kumite, submission wrestling and Brazilian Ju Jutsu. They have all been great learning environments and a hard test. No room for ego's, grades or status in these contests!

As much as I have enjoyed this we must not forget that MMA is still a sport, a tough one granted but still a sport. It is not a street fight and it doesn't necessarily prepare you for all-out close quarter combat or street self-defence! Sure it can help in many ways but the mindset for contest no matter how limited, is not the same as fighting for you life.

When I teach the two aspects of MMA and self-defence/street combat I try to make people aware they are two different worlds and being proficient in MMA or NHB fighting does not mean you could cut it in a street situation.

We must not get confused or brain washed. The two environments are completely different in many ways and if you want to train for both you must adapt and change aspects of your training and mind set totally.

MMA	Street Combat
Set rules (Even if limited).	No rules what so ever, non-existent.
Known opponent.	99% of time, totally unknown.
Known environment. not suitable for fighting (space, surfaces, lighting).	Environment un-chosen and certainly not suitable for fighting (space, surfaces, lighting).
Opponent same weight.	Opponent can be any age, shape or size.
You will know techniques that can and can't be used.	Attacker will be unpredictable, and will use everything, including weapons.
9 times out of 10 fights will be with gloves on	You may find yourself in your best suit or an overcoat and wellies!
and no illegal techniques.	Fights will be bare-knuckled, expect biting, eye gouging and groin shots.
Submission techniques will be concluded with a 'tap out'.	Any technique will be taken to it's conclusion, whether it be a broken limb or collapsed windpipe
Time limit to fights.	No time limit. It will go on until it ends.
Referee to see fair play.	Just you and your attacker(s).
Fight starts from sparring.	Fight will start by a pre-emptive shot.
Fighters will be of sound mind and body.	Your attacker could be fuelled by alcohol or drugs making him immensely strong and impervious to pain and totally unpredictable.
You will be fighting for a medal or trophy.	You will be fighting for you life.

Take a look at this chart and read through the differences of each and then ask yourself will your MMA be enough to see you through in any situation.

The list is no means exhaustive but it should give you an idea of the major differences. You can certainly adapt your training but you will have to work hard to simulate this in the training hall.

Obviously safety is essential in training and you can't go completely 'all out' but you can simulate scenarios and ideas to give you a good idea of what it's all about.

Street fights don't start with sparring up. Most street fighters work the pre-emptive shot and if you aren't switched on you will be out of the fight before you are in it! Street predators work behind cunning, guile, dialogue and the sucker punch. You can be a victim at anytime. It won't be when you're warmed up, stretched and in the frame of mind to have a go. It can happen when you are walking out of a restaurant with your partner, at the park with your kids, when you are cold, tired, wet or under the weather, getting in and out of your car or on a stairwell. If you go to the floor, you will be stamped and kicked un-mercifully by one or more parties. You may be attacked with a knife, a glass, a baseball bat or firearm.

Grappling with a weapon or with multiple opponents is suicidal. Falling or rolling around on a hard and uncompromising pavement is a world apart from a soft training mat.

You can be attacked in bad light or twilight where you cannot see your opponent clearly. Your sight may be impeded by a handful of dust thrown in your face, a glass of spirit or ammonia spray (a modern favourite in some circles). Your breathing may be impaired by choking with your own tie, being suffocated by a plastic bag or ducked under water. All of the above things have happened in street situations and worse. Unless you take this on board and train for it, you are not training for the street and MMA will not overlap into this hostile, scary and unpredictable environment. I have worked in, trained and experienced the above scenarios; they are a world apart from sports contests.

So how can you train for this? Well Geoff Thompson had the right idea with his animal day sessions. The environment, conditions and techniques were worked to simulate street reality.

Try starting scenarios with verbal aggression, pushing, shoving and then a pre-emptive shot, then fight from there.

Let the fight start with one opponent then bring one or more in at any given time. Train in full street clothes to feel their restrictions. Litter your mats with objects and obstacles e.g. bags, shoes, weapons, water bottles, pads, etc, so that you haven't got a clear area. Try grappling on grass or concrete (be careful). Switch the lights off and grapple against a weapon. To simulate grappling with somebody on drugs do this by firstly working 3 x 2 minute rounds on the focus mitts or the pads to become fatigued, then grapple a fresh partner or do the same and fight three partners in a row.

You must drill being grabbed from front, side and rear in all manners. Drill being punched, kicked, kneed, head butted, bitten and stomped and against all manner of weapons. Drill in cramped and confined places. Drill sitting down, kneeling down, pushed against a wall and so on. Practise pre-emptive shots; learn about line-ups, action triggers, combat distances, knockout shots, power striking and fear control and all the other unpredictability's of the street. Try simulated grappling or being attacked whilst in a bed. The soft mattress, tangle of sheets or a pillow over your face is a frightening situation.

A good doorman, bodyguard or security personnel don't have to indulge in MMA to be capable of defending themselves on the street. Their mindset, outlook and needs are totally different.

Awesome street fighters like Roy Shaw and the late Lennie McLean who were both good boxers have said on more than one occasion "Fighting in the ring and on the cobbles are two different things" and they trained for both. Also check out Geoff Thompsons 'Watch my back' to learn the differences if you don't already know. My own book 'Grappling with Reality' explicitly explores the difference between sport and combat grappling.
I have played devils advocate here because I practise street combat techniques and I have taught these principles to many door security staff, army and police, as well as the general public and have done so for many years but I am also a great lover of MMA. Competing in it, coaching it and watching and supporting it. I have met many fantastic people through the MMA scene and hope to go on doing so. Many of these people could easily make the transition into any arena, as they are natural fighters.

But I feel new comers arriving into martial arts who have watched a few UFC or MMA videos think it is the last word on combat and being able to defend yourself. MMA contest is a great sport and one for fighters to test themselves in a limited rules environment. It is real and it is hard but when all is said and done it is a sport. I would like to think those instructors are emphasising this point and that they can distinguish the difference between the two, and know where some aspects may merge together. Lets get Real

Recently I wrote an article in Fighters explaining and breaking down the difference between MMA and NHB fighting and reality techniques for the street. I am amazed through my travels and information gleaned from the Internet that a lot of people out there in the martial arts believe that MMA and street reality combat are one and the same thing!

Please don't confuse the two arenas, as they are totally different environments, with a completely different set of principles and agenda. I cannot emphasise this point enough and I would like to enlarge on the last article, to try and hammer this critical and often misunderstood point home.

Firstly, as I mentioned last time around, I am a massive fan of MMA competition. I have followed its development from the early UFC days right the way through to the present. It has developed and improved in leaps and bounds, due to the hard work of certain individuals who have gone to great lengths to make it an acceptable sport here in the UK and across the globe.

It is a hard sport, a reality sport, but it is still at the end of the day sport. It has rules (yes limited), it has a referee, rounds, time allotted and prize money or trophies, it's a sport!

My students and I have been heavily involved in MMA competition for the last few years and have experienced all it has to offer. It's a great pressure test for anybody wanting to try out their skills. I have met some great people and fighters over that time and enjoyed myself immensely, but I do get a little annoyed when some people say that MMA techniques are all that you need to protect yourself in a street situation. This is complete and utter rubbish!

Over the considerable years that I have been involved in the martial arts I have met, trained and worked with some of the premier self-protection experts in the UK. Men like Geoff Thompson, Peter Consterdine, Dave Turton, Jamie O'Keefe, Gary Spiers, Dave Turton and many more. None of these men are MMA or NHB competitors but if I wanted to know the reality of a street situation or personal security training I would be knocking on their doors – not on the door of a MMA champion.

What is street defence? How can we interpret it all? How do you view it?

It's certainly not, 'Karate in Jeans', as all the good self-defence books of the 70s and 80s made it out to be.

Are self-defence techniques swapping your Gi for combat fatigues or a tracksuit, and going outside and performing the same moves you would in a competition or dojo situation? Many presume it is exactly that! I have heard statements to the effect of, 'I would take my attacker straight down on the floor, pin him and then break his arm, no problem. That's my best move and they wouldn't be able to stop me!' I've got news for that person; start finding a different technique to work on, fast!

Self defence or personal security scenarios can be on a sliding scale from mildly dangerous to extremely dangerous or life threatening. When we go up the scale fighting for your life and being in a life-threatening situation is not MMA.

If I compete in MMA competition I know I'm not going to die. Unless some extreme fluke of circumstances was involved I will walk away or maybe carried away in one piece! Do you doubt that statement? Look at how many UFC, Extreme Fighting, Cage fighting, NHB and MMA competitions there have been in the past six or seven years, literally thousands and only a couple of fatalities have been reported in all that time, why? Because it's a sport. It's not life or death. In life or death people resort to extreme and deadly measures. Look at the Trade Centre terrorists' attacks in the USA. If you were in one of those hijacked planes confronted by three or more crazed terrorists and you knew you were going to die, what attack technique would you have applied from the MMA scene? A double leg takedown, in the narrow confines of a plane aisle?

Grappled and attempted to arm bar a knife wielding maniac with a couple of more friends ready to slash you to ribbons while you were doing it?
Think hard; this is the reality of real world self-protection, not ring sport. For situations like that you will need a different mental and physical programming that goes beyond throwing a few punches and kicks and being able to grapple. Being able to have a 'fight' won't cut it either. There are graveyards full of individuals that could have a fight!

Read the papers in the last few months and see the atrocities that human beings inflict upon each other, including the man stabbed to death for confronting car thieves, and the guy kicked to death after being pulled out of his car by a gang. Kids being battered senselessly for their mobile phones. People being car-jacked, dragged from vehicles, beaten and stabbed. These things didn't happen in New York, the Bronx or the Middle East, this was here in the UK. This is happening here and now! Now will your techniques and mind-set stand up to that sort of brutality?

Most street attacks are not perpetrated by one individual. Nor are they going to be stand up sparring matches. Most people don't realise they are in a street fight until somebody has sucker punched them or stuck a glass in their face. Very few street attackers want a stand up, drag 'em out encounter. They will close the gap with cunning dialogue, smile at you, and offer to shake your hand and then blast you off the planet! Real situations don't come from one on one sparring: it's more than one, knives are involved and worse. Go to the floor with two individuals and you will have problems. If you don't train in threat awareness, threat assessment, the fence, action triggers and pre-emptive shots you will fall foul to a street predator. Forget what a great punch, kick or strike you've got, forget how great a take-down or submission artist you are, you won't have time to use any of this. Let me emphasise the point again street combat is not a stand up sparring or a boxing match or MMA competition.

You can be attacked when you least feel like fighting. Like when you're out having a meal with your family or running back to your car, head down shielded against the wind and rain. When you have had too much to drink, when you feel ill or are carrying an injury.

You won't be fighting when you're all warmed up, stretched out, sweating and ready to kick off. Normally it's when we least expect or want it and then it is all so different.

Self-survival and MMA competition is the difference between swimming in the rough and cold ocean and swimming in a swimming pool. Although in a swimming pool you have an element of danger from drowning, nine times out of ten you can reach out and touch the side. In the other situation in the ocean it can be a desperately lonely and frightening, and above all life threatening.

Forget what style you train in and what's better – a Thai kick or a Judo throw. It's down to a different mind-set and realisation of what you are up against. You would need different tactics and strategies, and be able to adapt your techniques for a whole contrasting scenario completely. It's not to say MMA techniques won't work but you have got to change their approach, you don't want to end up bringing a knife to a gunfight!

Now there are many who have made the transition from combat self defence to MMA or from MMA to combat self defence, simply because they understood the difference in the arena and circumstances, but many others though are totally convinced that MMA is the be all and end all when it comes to self defence. This is a conceited and dangerous attitude.
As I mentioned earlier don't be under the illusion that a street attack is going to always come from the front. Many MMA stylists that talk about street self-defence are presuming attackers will approach just as they will in the Contest Square, ring or cage. This is not true. You can discuss the merits of a Thai thigh kick or a Taiotoshi throw (both excellent techniques) but they will be of no value when you are crammed inside a phone booth or car seat with a knife shoved under your nose. These are real world attack scenarios.

If you aren't training for these things, you're not training for the street! Let's not have the narrow-minded attitude that every situation in the street is a guy 'having' a go at you down the pub. Street attacks are unpredictable, perpetrated by unpredictable people, not trained fighters with trained responses.

Believe me, I speak from experience, there are guys out there who will not care how many titles, belts, trophies or fights you have won, they will carve you up with a machete, strike your head with a hammer or put a chair over your back without a moment's hesitation or worry. The guys aren't hard, they are bloody dangerous, and they have no sense of fair play whatsoever.

Your mind-set for dealing with these individuals is totally different to entering the ring for a MMA contest. Wherever I have fought MMA I didn't hate my opponent and I certainly didn't go in there with the intent to main or grievously harm them. I view it as a game, a hard game but not life threatening. If it were life threatening, any restraining, rules or sportsmanship would have gone out of the window. I would have pre-emptively hit my opponent as we touched gloves in the middle and proceeded to bite and gouge lumps out of him before choking him. That's not acceptable in MMA and quite rightly so but that's 'real combat' not sport. Let's please not confuse them for a minute, otherwise it could be costly.

Chapter 22
Random Thoughts

(Questions and Answers)

As I am writing this book and trying to remember different points in my training, thought and memories come and go. Random musings, suddenly enter my head, that have no particular pattern but need to be addressed. I will attempt to put these thought in some order.

Associations

I have often been asked why I never started up my own Association. Well, in answer to this I find the more you expand the harder you have to work to maintain student's standards and oversee that your system or ideas are being adhered to in the correct manner. By running my own small group of clubs I can teach and oversee them all without much problem, plus I have trained a certain number of instructors who are capable of teaching and following my chosen art the way I see it. This close knit environment means standards are high. For instance if I ran an Association here in Bristol and took on clubs in say Scotland, Manchester and Liverpool, unless I could get to these places and regularly monitor progress I have no say or control over those clubs and students. I can see the financial attraction of taking on board a club with a hundred members, the membership fees alone would be great business but I can't vet the clubs or instructors, it would be wrong to take on that club on the strength of a phone call. You see if this club is under your banner and name and if it's not up to standard or being run in a professional manner, it comes back on you. Particularly in this day and age with so much MMA's and full contact training you need to know things are being run safely. When you widen your net, financially you may reap the benefits but you lose a certain degree of control, which I don't like. On running a club and teaching, it is a vast learning curve. The old saying the journey is more beneficial than the destination is a true one. I have learnt masses along the way and have much experience on how to keep a class successful and also profitable if its your living without 'selling out'.

Art of Coaching

When I first started teaching it was not as a living so I didn't unduly worry how many people came and trained or how many dropped out. I taught one way, hard and uncompromising. It was a take or leave it attitude. What I found was that you always ended up with a small hardcore group of trainers and many others flitting in and out on the periphery. You had serious Martial artists and recreational ones. I was only interested in people who were going to give 100%, like if they didn't, I wouldn't drag them along. Of course my classes were pretty small and not really expanding because I wouldn't compromise. I didn't want to water down my techniques or change my teaching. When I went professional I realised if I didn't alter my methods I wouldn't survive and would not make even a decent living. So I designed classes for different peoples needs. I would have Combat Ju Jutsu classes for syllabus work for grading etc, where the training is always lively but not hardcore. In these classes I built up people's fitness, confidence and technique one step at a time rather than chucking them in the deep end. I also had classes for advanced students and instructors and also classes for hard sparring, grappling, realistic street combat and MMA. The guys who thrived on hard training and contact training knew where to come. The other classes were like a filter system to gradually encourage others into the hardcore lessons, or if they didn't want to I wouldn't push them. This has been a highly successful method for me, as I realised over the years not everybody is in Martial Arts for the same reason. You have to find out what they want and try to cater for them. By doing it this the way I have. Also, I haven't had to compromise my art or water it down. I have found the right balance. Also I am a great believer in not putting all your eggs in one basket. Whatever type of training that is currently flavour of the month can and will suddenly change.

I train, teach and compete MMA, but also retain teaching in Combat Ju Jutsu and self-protection. Having more than one string to the bow can be handy but I have had to work hard to gain all this knowledge. You certainly don't want to be Jack of all trades and Master of none. I have been fortunate in the fact that Ju Jutsu has always been a multi faceted art where I have trained in all ranges which amounts to vast knowledge. Cross training and hybrid training are for me just an extension of my art. My open mindedness has held me in good stead for the modern Martial Arts scene although I started training nearly 30 years previously.

I have been lucky not to get stuck in my ways or let my art become a monkey on my back that I have to carry, as some others have found to their cost.

I agree very much with the cross training principle but I also agree you should have a solid base art to build on and been training in it for some years. Too many young guys today are training in Boxing, JKD, Thai, Ju Jutsu, Savate, and Sambo. This is virtually an impossible task if you want to be proficient in any of them. Remember the saying the 'Fox that chases two rabbits at once, catches none!' Be careful. Yes, there is so much more variety out there now in the Martial Arts world. The beginner is spoiled for choice. Clubs are popping up just about everywhere and you have a myriad of styles. There are first class instructors on the seminar circuit from the world over. You also have videos, CD, DVD and Internet to help boost training. You are all lucky but beware chasing too many goals at the same time.

When I first started training as I mentioned Kung Fu was the 'in' style but the clubs were few and far. You had to keep your ear to the ground, I found out about them and then you had a job to track them down. Remember when I first wanted Ju Jutsu there was none in my hometown or within a 50 mile radius of it. Now Ju Jutsu clubs are everywhere. Also books were the only source of additional instruction and some of these were very poor or just basics. This day and age it's the skies the limit. If you are dedicated you will learn much more and in half the time that the old stagers and veterans did. God, I sound like one of the 'four Yorkshiremen' in that Monty Python sketch.' in my day.......!

The Black Belt today

Does a black belt hold any value in this day and age? This is always a good subject for debate.

In these days of MMA and NHB fighting we don't see much of the traditional black belt worn and for today's young and rising stars of the Martial Arts world a black belt doesn't seem to be at the top of their list of priorities. Certainly when I was a youthful Martial Artist my goal was a black belt achievement. But in some ways over the years it has been de-valued by greedy money orientated Associations that gave out these belts like smarties. It seemed at one stage everybody I met had a black belt in one art or another. The black belt in some quarters became a joke.

In the event of the grappling explosion and reality fight scene, many a black belt were taken down to earth by lesser grades that could have a fight. People were drawing conclusions from this and coming up with the answer that the black belt was infact worthless. My thoughts on this are as follows. Firstly a black belt is an individual and personal thing. What it means to you, how you carry it and what you do with it is down to that individual. Some arts you can receive a black belt for your technical ability and understanding of the system without ever having to test yourself. A lot of Martial Arts have little or no combat value, others do, it will depend what art you have come from and what you achieved the black belt for. A black belt certainly doesn't mean you're an 'expert' or a master fighter. That idea has been sold to the public by the media. It does show a measure though of your achievements within your chosen systems. It's the same with any job, pursuit, sport or pastime; you will always have awards and marks of your achievements or dedication to that pursuit, why should the Martial Arts be any different.

Let's be realistic, can a sixty five-year-old 8th Dan compete against a twenty three-year-old blue belt in a contest? Answer very unlikely, but does that mean that man has nothing to offer? Of course not. He can offer vast experience and knowledge that he can pass on to the younger men and coach and groom him. Look at some of boxings greatest coaches, some were either poor or average fighters themselves but they had a talent to coach. Are they thought any less of for that?

Dan grades in Martial Arts reflect the time you have given to your system and the knowledge you have achieved not whether you are a 'karate killer' or not. I do feel though that every black belt has a responsibility to themselves to be a good or a poor black belt. Some reach the high level, take their foot off the pedal and relax back on their achievements; others will see it as another rung on the ladder and adjust accordingly.

My advice is if you grade for belts in a syllabus, make the syllabus full and challenging and make sure people earn that belt honestly. Gaining black belts in two years to me is not an option.

That span of time will not give you the knowledge or experience to carry that grade. If certain quarters believe the black belt is worthless, it is down to instructors to make sure it isn't and give it back the status it deserves, but at the same time clarify what it signifies and what it doesn't.

Heroes and Influences

My heroes and influences in the Martial Arts have been many and also varied, depending on the stage I was at in my career. For anybody who started Martial Arts in the 70's, Bruce Lee has to be a massive influence and a hero. The image of this icon on the front of a magazine today some 25 plus years after his untimely death can still boost it's sales. His films are still avidly watched over and over and they always seem to be a new book in the offering about his life. This goes to show what a phenomenal influence he was and still is so many years on down the line. Stripping away all the razzmatazz and bullshit about him, he truly was a man ahead of his time in the Martial Arts. In the 60's he was training and experimenting with what we know today forty years on as cross training and mixed Martial Arts. If he were alive today I'm sure he would fully support the MMA scene and been a big part of it. I believe this was his vision for Martial Arts training.

One of my first instructors John Bennett is a man I greatly respect. He took time with me to give me the best of instruction but also advice when I was a young man. He became a close friend and I admired his straight forward manner, honesty and integrity. Where you're a 'young man' in your teens, you think you know it all and nobody can tell you anything. Well I always had time to listen to John and heed his advice. It takes a special kind of person to do this and that was John. A little man in stature but a big, big influence.

I have always been a big boxing fan and in the 1980's men like Hagler, Leonard, Duran and Hearns were my boxing heroes. Thomas the 'hitman' Hearns particularly was my favourite, I even named my oldest boy, Thomas after him.Hearns was a legend at welter, light middle, middle, super middle and light heavy, five world titles! I have never seen a faster or more accurate jab than the 'hitmans' and although we bear no resemblance body wise I tried hard to emulate his moves. Duran was also a hero, a fantastic and under ratedboxer, known more for his brawling techniques. A superb fighter and body puncher. These men inspired me greatly as I was training.

Heading towards modern times I loved to watch Julio Caesar Chavez fight. He could have fought his bouts in a telephone box. He was a relentless boxer/puncher and one of the cruellest body punchers in the world.

Evander Holyfield is also a hero of mine. I have never known a more dedicated boxer, with such strong belief in himself. He defied critics so many times and pulled off unbelievable results. Also an incredibly humble man, a true champ.

In the big wide world of Martial Arts, I have immense respect for Royce Gracie. He put the world of MMA's on the map with superb technical performance of Ju Jutsu. People have been too quick to knock 'this man' but let's remember he won three UFC's when you had to fight three or four times on the trot. Most of his victories were against bigger and stronger men. Plus let's also remember he wasn't the best of the greatest clan. He took the Gracie challenge squarely on his shoulders and must have been under un-believable pressure to uphold his families' honour. He is a true Martial Arts warrior and in my eyes a hero.

Another Martial Artist I highly rate is Marco Lalo. This guy has got to be one of the hardest trainers in the world, plus a superb technician not only in the striking and kicking arts but also grappling. His training tapes are fantastic and motivational. Finally no round up of inspirational men would be complete without my friend Geoff Thompson. I have never hid my admiration for this man and he has constantly inspired me to greater things. Geoff is a man who whilst climbing the ladder of success, has always got time to reach out and help others up a few more rungs. This is the mark of a great person. What I admire most about Geoff is, he was the first Martial Artist who openly in public admitted it was alright to be scared and feel fear and he spoke quite candidly about this. He made a whole lot of people feel better about themselves, when he disclosed it.

Up to that time Martial Artists were all totally machismo. No fear, no pain, indestructible and immovable. None would admit to fear as they would feel it was a sign of weakness, so all others in their wake followed suit.

Geoff changed all this and opened many new doors and horizons for a lot people. He has booked his place in Martial Arts history and I am proud to be his mate. There are many others in the Martial Arts I respect, admire and like, to many to list but the people I have previously mentioned are high on my list.

What do you hate in Martial Arts?

I don't like how hard working, professional and highly proficient Martial Artists are not treated like other good sports people or achievers in their field. They do not get the recognition or financial benefits others do. It is an undersold and under rated profession, that requires immense dedication and training to reach high standards.

As you may have guessed one of my pet hates are self - important instructors, who really are legend in their own minds. The Martial Arts world is littered with these characters.

I have always been a firm believer in practise what you preach and in the same token preach what you practise. If I tell you I have experienced boxing, full contact training, hard submission grappling and Vale Tudo, I have and I will teach from those experiences. If I put you through an arduous programme of conditioning and exercise it will be nothing I haven't experienced, that's how I am.

I will not tell tall tales, exaggerate the truth or make out I'm something I'm not, what you see is what you get. I don't class myself as a master but I have got vast knowledge and experience in the Martial Arts and I don't consider myself to be a premier fighter or Ninja killer turtle, but I have talked the talk and walked the walk. For all I have achieved, I know there are others who have achieved more and I am not so wrapped up in my own abilities that I can't learn from somebody else. I hate frauds, bullshitters and those that promise but don't deliver.

Dedication and Commitment

I am a great believer in both of the above mentioned things. I have always tried to give a 100% in my training or teaching and I respect others that do the same. In my time I have been let down on many occasions by students who could not show the desire or commitment to push themselves that little bit further. Or individuals who took but couldn't return the favour and give back. It saddens me that these people that I spent so much time and effort with so easily 'throw you into touch' when something more important comes along or when their enthusiasm begins to fade.

There are many times as a professional instructor I have wished I had had the night off or cringed at the thought of having to teach but I've carried on and done it and to the best of my ability and I don't think it's too much to ask for a bit of the same commitment back but sadly this isn't always the case.

I really do get 'pissed' with individuals telling me how they want to pass this grade or that grade or how they want to compete or how they will make an effort to get to certain classes and then let you down time and time again. I often wandered how many classes I would have if I had the same attitude and done this kind of thing myself!

The excuses I have heard over the years have been many about why a person isn't training or can't make it. Sure some re genuine others are laughable. I have heard so many that I now let them go through one ear and out the other. We can all find excuses for all our shortcomings, most come down to commitment and dedication.

Humbleness through Adversity

Those of you out there that have read 'Bad to the Bone' will know I went through periods of volatile behaviour in my life. Where I became an aggressive person and probably the type of person I hated but didn't realise. I have done and said things I regret now but I can't change the past but I can certainly shape the future. I realise my bursts of aggression were more than likely due to lack of security and the need to prove oneself. I think all young people go through this at one time or another. Without wishing to expand on the issues I have at one time or another experienced courtrooms and Police cells. I have been in court to give evidence, to be a character witness and to sit on a jury. I didn't relish any of the experiences and I certainly wouldn't want to be involved along those lines again if it could be avoided. You must learn from the traumas life can throw at you. Now I am in control and put that part of my character behind me. I have the ability to look at things more objectively now and the discipline from the Arts has given me that. The desire to prove myself in the physical sense is no know longer my sole function. There are many other things I wish to do and explore. Physically you can only do so much and go so far, mentally you can keep on growing forever.

Going to Ground?

I am often asked this question, 'How do I get better at ground grappling?' Now before I answer that question I only class myself as a fair ground grappler. I am by no means a master but in the last five years I have set aside adequate time from my other training to devote many hours to groundwork.

In my long career in Ju Jutsu I have been exposed to different types of groundwork for many years but it was all pretty basic and combat orientated. When the grappling fever hit the Martial Arts scene I saw there was much more to learn form this exciting and fascinating subject. My senior lads and myself started finding time to devote sessions to just floorwork. We would work through the basic pins first, gaining the skill to hold and control another opponent. Without this foundation skill, you can forget the armbars, leg locks and chokes, you just won't get them. Students are always in a hurry to learn the submissions and do not give enough time to pins. If you don't you will be like a surfer out in the sea trying to stand up on your board and each wave will keep knocking you back off. Position and control is everything. I like the mottos, 'Pin to win' and 'Position before submission'. We used to just work around these positions, moving from one to another sometimes for an hour before trying a submission.

We did the same with two or three submissions and just drilled them over and over to get a real feel for them and then add another one. Quality is definitely better than quantity.

Working the guard was the same, sometimes whole sessions just on your back. One man defending, one passing, over and over.

Reversing positions done in the same manner, sweeps and combinations follow with the same approach.

Compliant grappling, fifty- percent grappling and full out matches. Grappling in a Gi, T-shirt, no top and submission and Vale Tudo and all out combat grappling.

Sometimes we would just roll and grapple up to 45 mins to an hour, non-stop. We just seemed to be on the floor all the time. If you want to be good you have got to be doing this stuff as often as humanly as possible. My senior lads and myself have devoted years to this skill alone never mind all the other aspect we train in. This requires one hell of a lot of dedication and determination. This is not a five-minute wonder, you have got to really want it and develop a level of skill that gives you confidence and skill.

Most people do not practice enough or in a structured and progressive manner, so they struggle to improve.

I feel some do not realise the effort and time you need to dedicate to become proficient. You have to drill until you can do the moves in your sleep and you become sick of actually practising them, then you know your getting somewhere. So hit the mat and get training. Don't dabble, master it!

How long will it take me to become good at a Martial Art?

Wow, what a question. How long is a piece of string? The quick answer to this is basically you only get out what you put in. I have so many people come to me and comment, "I don't seem to be progressing" or "Do you think I'm ready for my next grading?" I feel like saying your not progressing because you don't train often enough. You go missing for weeks on end and then come back and expect to get things right, it just won't happen. When you do train you don't put in enough effort or try hard enough, you don't come to the sessions that matter. You won't make the sacrifices.

I know not everybody has the same goals in Martial Arts but if you want to get good in something you have got to practice it as often as possible and give it your all.

There is no time limit to proficiency. Some people are naturals and pick it up quite quickly others struggle and take longer. But all can achieve, you have got to put in the work.

The grade or the belt means nothing if it has been given to you, it carries no weight or substance, you have to earn it and go through the process, there are no short cuts but your dedication and effort can speed you along.

In my system the belts are earned, never given, nobody can buy them either, this why as mentioned before I don't run associations this way I can monitor and keep a personal eye on standards.

Where do you see Martial Arts going in the future?

I think the face of Martial Arts has changed forever when the cross training and mixed Martial Arts hit the scene. This type of training broke down a lot of mystery and mystic about Martial Arts and presented a truer and new picture. I think this type of training is here to stay but other arts and aspects of training will also last the course.

In the wake of the twin towers disaster on September 11th 2001, the USA has now turned their attention to realistic personal training again. Combat masters and Street survival experts are in demand to teach self-protection and close personal defence methods. The people of America are united in fighting back against terrorists and crime whether it is on a huge scale or a personal one. Unfortunately there will always be the need for this type of training, as violence is an everyday occurrence in these modern times.

This side of my training I always have demand for and I will never give up teaching this aspect of my art. The atrocities of September 11th touched us all and reached out to us. On a personal note two weeks before the horrific incident my family and I stood outside the Trade Centre marvelling at its vastness, we were that close to a possible tragedy.

Although traditional Martial Arts will have a place in our society, I think their influence will be no where as big as they were in past times. The fighting arts have been around as long as man and they will still be around after I have gone. Today's Martial Artist has a wealth of information at hand and a fresh new openness about training that they should seize and make the most of while it's here.

'Have have you enjoyed your experiences in the MMA arena?

Yes, I have, very much. I am glad I still could have a bite of the cherry so to speak and be involved with it all.

I must admit the MMA came ten years to late for me and I know I would have been more heavily involved and competing regularly. Having said that I still got the chance at the tail end of my competitive career to have a go. As I've mentioned previously just to have kept myself in shape and be conditioned enough to mix it with young, up and coming fighters has pleased me greatly and proved all my hard years of training had not been a waste. Not having been a big sport Martial Artist or a man who was used to fighting in a rule orientated structure, I have enjoyed the experience and find the whole MMA scene exciting and a breath of fresh air. I hope I can go on to coach further champions. My two top competitors Matt Sperring and Ross MacKenzie have the potential to both be champions in this field. Although the 'old boy' here can still give them both a run for their money even now. Also I have found some great young lads ready to compete soon and I have a lot of hope in them.

‘What lessons have you learnt from MMA?

I have learnt that no one system has all the answers in MMA contest. I originally thought my Ju Jutsu background would be enough and although I could fight stand up and on the floor I found out I needed to add and refine these skills. I took much from Western boxing, Muay Thai, Wrestling and submission shooto to round out certain skills and be more prepared for this extreme environment. Fighting skilled athletics is completely different to fighting unskilled and untrained opponents. These top boys are mega fit, strong, sharp and technically good, they are doing this all of the time. Totally different to a pub brawler. It takes a lot of bottle to go one to one in the ring or cage.

When you fight you need a game plan and strategy, it’s not just about going in there and having a go, not if you want to be good at it. Once you develop a game plan you stick to it. A good coach and trainer is essential. Rob Cannon was absolutely priceless in helping me prepare for my bigger fights.

You have to also develop ring craft or cage craft! Experienced pros have this and they feel at home in this environment. You need to prepare with time in a ring or similar.

Repetition of solid basic techniques is the foundation for success. It’s not how much you know it’s how good you are with what you’ve got. Drill, drill, drill is the key over and over under pressure until you can pull off the strike combo, takedown or submission. Also lots of clinch work is essential and not to be over looked or under estimated.

The MMA or NHB is a complete system in itself and the more I done it, the more I realised you have to totally devote yourself to this training on a daily basis to become good at it. Being able to have a fight isn’t enough. The top pros are professional athletes who deserve respect.

Fitness is a big factor, fighting two, three or more five minute rounds requires great stamina and you have to train like crazy and be committed. Sure, you might finish the fight in 20 seconds or it might be 10 minutes. Real fighting at this level and pace is totally exhausting for a twenty-year-old let alone for a guy of forty, it’s extreme. I am glad to say my fitness training over the years held me in good stead.

Finally I meet some excellent fighters but who are also gentlemen. Out of the fight arena they were humble, funny and down to earth, fortunately only a small amount I encountered were un-sportsmanlike or bad losers.

Guys to watch in this field are the likes of Paul Jenkins, Cassan Hipkiss, Alex Owen and Ross Petifer, amongst others. All are great fighters..All the events I have been to have been first class and I would like to praise all promoters and organisers especially local guys like Dale (ML Sports) and Justin (Martial Mania). Well done.

Open mindedness and hunger to learn

I had found that no matter how long you devote yourself to a chosen activity or sport there is always something new or different to learn. Obviously that only applies though if you are prepared to learn and want to explore new horizons. It's easy to sit in your comfort zone and not reach outside of it. For many instructors, they will sit back on their grades, reputations or past glories and be contest with this or won't push themselves further to have a peek over the next hill and see what's there.

I have always been excited with the changes in the Martial Arts world and tried to be in there on the cutting edge of what's new. Rather than ridicule or slag off 'new' I have tried to embrace it and explore it and then be able to give an informed opinion. I would not have survived this long if I had not adapted this point of view. I have been here from the early days of the Bruce Lee Kung Fu craze and am still actively involved and training in today's MMA revolution. There has not been a time I haven't been on the mats and training and trying to better myself. I am not too proud or egotistic to go and learn off anybody I feel can teach me, whether they are a lower grade than me or not.

As mentioned previously there are too many instructors out there who are sitting on self imposed pedestals. They have been elevated to the heady heights of master and their heads are firmly planted in the clouds. They believe their own hype. The problem is that the foundation of the pedestal is a shaky one. Many instructors have long since given up the ideal of actually training themselves and believe their credentials or Dan grades will make everything alright. They turn up at seminars and stand on the outside of the mat but don't get on to participate in any shape or form. I have witnessed on seminars stood on the edge of a mat area chatting and then breeze on to demonstrate a technique with their top student. They will 'bounce' them all over the place half a dozen times and then tell class to try it themselves. They then strut off again lost in their self important. They are not remotely interested whether the class has grasped the technique or can execute it. All they re concerned with is showing them how 'awesome' they are and taking the money!

Cynical? You bet! This has gone on for years, I could name names but I want to avoid any lawsuits! I can honestly say if I have been paid to teach a seminar I will do my utmost to impart my knowledge on the students and give them something worthwhile to take home with them. When I have been on a seminar and great men like Neil Adams or John Machado have come over and spent personal time helping me correct or improve a technique, it is long remembered and appreciated.

I don't want people just to remember me for my techniques. I want them to remember my teaching, my approach and my enthusiasm for them to learn. I love teaching Martial Arts but I also love training in them. There is not a week that goes by when I 'm not working out with my students, sparring, grappling etc. I am a hands on instructor. I am always on the mat, which is my domain; it's what I do best. On the mats I can switch on and perform. Just like an actor or singer in front of a camera or walking onto a stage. It's where they belong and come into their own. The mats are my stage and I want to be active on them as long as possible. If you don't train regularly you lose your edge, sharpness and hunger and you will be fooling yourself if you think other wise. Obviously as you get older you can't do what you did when you were in your twenties but there is no reason to give up actively training altogether.

At present I personally train in three major sessions a week. Sunday mornings are the hardest. They are always a mental and physical battle to attend and I know what's coming. It is easy to wake up and want to pull the duvet back over your head and go to sleep but you make yourself get up and go for it! The sessions are heavy and demanding and I have been doing these constantly for the last six years. The class evolves around hard conditioning, impact pad work, sparring in boxing, kick boxing, grappling and Vale Tudo. They are extreme and take pressure testing to the limit.

Tuesday evening is a more basic MMA/Vale Tudo class where the tempo isn't as fast, but you do loads and loads of drilling.

Thursdays I train private one to one as well as usually getting an hour of bag work in myself. Thursday I can train two or three hours in the morning and may be have to train in the evening again.

This is my Martial Arts training and I will do a couple of gym sessions as well on top of this, the rest of the week I am teaching. It is a heavy schedule and sometimes you get jaded and very sore. You have got to find a fine line of balance otherwise you can burn out. As I have mentioned previously it doesn't get any easier as you advance in age.

I do enjoy the training but sometimes it can be a love/hate relationship and you really have to 'steel yourself' to train. Learning to train smarter as you get older is essential.

I still get plenty of sparring in but I do find some of the youngsters or less experienced will go at it,' like a bull in a china shop'. If you agree on a steady spar that's what I will stick with, I can control my adrenalin and technique to whatever level that is required. I have sparred with 'lads' and they have come straight in 'bang' and took a liberty and you think 'hang on what's all this, I though we were going steady'. You have to be abide by the rules put down and have respect. I don't want to have to end up fighting everybody. I have done too much of this and I don't want to have to prove myself every session. When people have taken advantage I have had to change gear and give them a 'dig' or slam on a choke but I get frustrated that it had to go to this when all you were meant to be doing was have a steady spar or roll. I suppose some want to make a name for themselves and don't realise that you might not be going full throttle. Over the years I have responded to this and punished some people but afterwards haven't felt particularly proud. My motto is that I will not take advantage or liberties with anyone unless they do it to me and then I will do what I have to do to defend myself and I mean anything! There are a lot of bullies in this game that like dishing it out but not taking it. I don't like bullying or arrogance. I know with some guys it can be just youthful enthusiasm but others they have a nasty streak and enjoy hurting people. If you spar lay down the ground rules first and both stick to them, then you will not have problems.

I feel one reason that some high grade instructors don't participate on the mats is for fear of losing face or being humbled by a lesser grade. I have competed, grappled and sparred with many people and been beaten and humbled by lads I know who have half my experiences or grades but it didn't faze me or stop me from trying again. In the same token I have beaten good people but that's the way it goes, swings and roundabouts. The man who hasn't lost hasn't competed. There are so many people out there spouting on about real training, reality combat, etc and some have never experienced any or just stood on the edge of the pool, frightened to dip their toe in! I promise you whatever I speak about or have an opinion on I have experienced, when this book was mentioned a life on the mats, I meant it totally. My life has been on the mats. If there was ever a time I didn't walk into a Dojo or training hall I wouldn't feel right.

Now with what I have commented on here, I am not trying to impress on you the reader I am the best Martial Artist in the country or even my home town, I am just stating to achieve anything in life you must be true and experience it. In Bristol my home town I have great fellow Martial Artists and fighting champions like Shaun Viera, Martin Herd,, John Munden ,Andy and Chris Davies and Ross Hale amongst others. Although they are from different arts and backgrounds the common link they all have are that they have put themselves on the line on numerous occasions to prove their skills. I admire them for this. They can talk the talk and walk the walk! They are not paper tigers or individuals who are living in a Martial Arts fantasy world, they are real but at the same time incredible humble men.

My good mates and fellow self protection instructors Alan Charlon and Darren Richardson (who is also a Sambo champ) are high graded and first class instructors in their own right but when I have taught on seminars they are always there on the mats training, that is respect and first class attitude. No egos. The strutting, snarling and posing brigade seem a joke in these men's presence.

Chapter 22

'On a Personal note'

This book has very much been about my experiences, thoughts and opinions on Martial Arts. Away from that arena I am a private person and don't usually mix the two. My family knows my love, passion and dedication for the arts and when it also became my living they accepted I would have to devote a large percentage of my time to them. But when I am away from training, teaching etc, my family gives me the balance in my life. Dealing with reality combat fills you sometimes with the loathing that one human being can inflict on another and you do get immersed in the dark side of human nature. My family is the light, the good side and the positive side and I count myself a lucky man to have this.

My kids have grown up with Martial Arts and they all practice Ju Jutsu. I haven't forced them into it, it was something they wanted to do. If at any time they don't want to train I will not stand in their way. I would just hope they devoted some time to keeping fit and practising basic self-defence skills, so that wherever they end up in the world, they would be safe and streetwise.

Tina, my wife has always supported my training and been a solid support for me when things have been good and bad. We went through some tough times when I first started out as a professional instructor and we had very little income coming in. We learned to live without many things and budgeted to do so. Through all this we kept the faith (isn't that a record) and never doubted that things would get better. She hasn't always agreed with some of things I've embarked on but never stood in my way. For this I am deeply grateful.

As mentioned away from the 'mats' I am not a Martial Arts bore. If I am in the company of fellow combat practitioners I can talk on the subject all night long. If I'm not I don't mention it unless somebody asks me about my work or past times. I have encountered too many 'Martial Artists' who go around trying to impress upon anybody who wants to listen, how deadly they are and how supremely skilled they may be. It wears thin in the end and I know how boring and utterly pathetic it sounds.

Also I find if a person who is not involved in the Martial Arts hears that you are, they still come out with the old cliché's 'I wouldn't want to meet you in a dark alley, '(why do they presume I would be in one), or 'I won't upset you then mate' (as if I was going to tear their throats out if I disagreed with them). It wears a bit thin sometimes. Plus I find many men suddenly put up their mental guard and subconsciously start posing because I presume they feel I'm a threat. This is why I keep quiet and try to avoid the subject.

Another classic remark will be,"Oh I used to do karate or whatever but I had to give it up because I hurt my back, or knee, or foot etc etc". There are oh so many fallen or would be warrior's on the planet. The excuses that get trotted out border from lame to highly ridiculous.

When I'm relaxing from training I love to read, I am a voracious reader and I always have a book on the go. Some reading I use to educate and inform myself, other to entertain. I like autobiographies and books in achievement or endurance through hardship. I find them inspirational and informative. If I'm on holiday and just want to totally unwind I may read horror fiction, which I have had an inkling for since childhood. Authors like Shaun Hudson and Richard Laymon are the top men in this field.

I have a great sense of humour and love comedy shows especially those that mirror real lives. Those really close to me know my wicked and dry humour well. Those that know me professionally though my Martial Arts etc will not see what I term as my alter ego. Normally I keep him well buried and in check while I'm at my 'job'. I am these days a disciplined performer who tries to be professional in his whole approach to his training and coaching, but every now and then when I am relaxed the 'old Kev' can appear, he can he funny but also dangerous that's why I keep him in check. Those who know me from old will know what I mean. There is a time for seriousness and damn hard work and a time for fun. These days I have the balance. When I'm 'at the office' so to speak (the training hall or gym is my office) I give a 100% in all I do and can be intense. I do the business, away from that I can chill out a bit.

I also like to get away to peaceful settings like the countryside or by the water. I find this helps me recharge the batteries and get away from the rush of city life. I have also got the travel bug within the last five years and would very much like to do more of this in the years to come.

Some years back I achieved a long time ambition to visit the USA. It was a wonderful experience. The West Coast is fabulous, a rich mixture of cultures and scenery, totally breath-taking. I have been fortunate enough to revisit the states twice more and I dream of seeing the whole fifty states, what a life times work!

Those of you who have read "Bad to the bone" will know two weeks prior to the terrible tragedy of September 11th, my family and I stood marvelling at the colossal size of the trade centre twin towers in New York. When the news broke weeks later of the devastation, death and mayhem, we were deeply affected by it all. We have friends and relations in America and I felt for them all. I am not into preaching politics or religion, I just know from my personal experiences I have found the American people and the American way of life fantastic and I wish them all my best.

If I were asked to give out some piece of advice to you the readers to learn from I would have to say in your life it is important to have goals. Goals, targets and destinations without them you wonder through life aimlessly, letting opportunity slip you by. You will not recognise progression and you will instead be wandering aimlessly.

It will be like being lost in a desert without a clue in what direction to head. As you get to the top of one sand dune, all you will see ahead are countless others. In the end you won't even bother climbing the dunes because you will know what will await you. You must plan your goals carefully and map them out so you know where you are heading and what you need to do, have purpose in your life. Don't be the sort of person who is looking forward to their summer holiday in February with nothing in between, or the person who eight o'clock Monday morning in work is already waiting for five o'clock Friday. Don't wish your life away; take something positive from each and every day.

About five years ago I decided that before every New Year I would sit down and write my goals for the coming year. Once they are on paper they are set and can be worked towards. Some goals were long term, large ones, which may take more than a year to achieve but at least I could start on them. Others were short term and quite achievable, whilst others were immediate goals, something that I could change about myself or my life straight away.

I also kept a diary of these goals, so that each day I could monitor my progress. Remember a small step in progress is better than none at all.

During the year whilst working towards those goals with targets and direction I was surprised at what could be achieved. It really works, but you must be single minded and dedicated to achieve. Take for example a man like Richard Branson, a self-made millionaire and more. People can be envious and jealous of his achievements but these didn't come overnight. From a young age he worked tirelessly through goals, direction, targets and great vision for what he wanted. He had hardship on the way and failure but he refused to give up and tried and tried again. As he completed one project with success he was onto another one straight away. His life story is an inspirational one. You may not have the goals that Branson has but it all works on the same basis. If you want to improve in an area of your life first you have got to accept that it needs improving and do a complete character X ray of yourself. It's not always pleasant but it has to be done.

I did this some 7 or 8 years ago and began to totally change myself for the better. I changed a lot of my bad habits, weaknesses and personality traits. I started to re-educate myself and set many goals in my Martial Arts career and private life. My reward was achievement in things I never though I could gain. I have met and associated with great people I otherwise wouldn't have met. I pushed myself to new levels of skill and ability in Martial Arts and basically became a better person. I also believe firmly in having time for others. What you give out you reap back two fold, somewhere along the line. In this day and age people have little or no time for others, it's a selfish society. Learn to give and doors will open for you and you will get much spiritual refreshment.

Whether you believe in God or a higher universal power or energy it doesn't matter. I believe something or someone is looking down on you and they will guide you and give you choices, it's what you do with those choices that determine how you live your life. Lastly remember your life is now, not tomorrow, next week, next month, next year. It is now!

So start working towards what you want out of it. You only get one shot and this is it. Some of my goals took five years to achieve but what a sense of fulfilment you get when they are reached. To some many of my goals may not seem great but to me each and everyone was significant. I came from very humble beginnings and worked relentlessly to better myself. Go on you can do whatever you want and be the person you want to be.

The formula is goals, targets, destinations, vision, belief, dedication, tenacity.

In memory of

In the chapter 'Aikido Years' I mention a former instructor who I referred to as 'Polish John'. It has recently come to my attention that John has suddenly passed away as a result of a virus having claimed his life within two weeks. This shocked and saddened me. He was well respected within the Aikido world and I wish to send my sincere sympathy to his family and friends. R.I.P.

Epilogue

This is one year on from my memorable fortieth birthday party. Two weeks previous on Sunday June 9th I was tempted yet again back into the competitive arena for a fight on the Ultimate Combat II. "The World Warriors" held at Chippenham. The fight card was promoted by ML Sports and sanctioned by the British Association of Mixed Martial Arts.

Early in the year I went to the first Ultimate Combat to view the show. I told myself if I watched it and decided I was no longer capable of competing at this level I would call it a day, but after the event I knew I had something left to give it a go.

Immediately after the show finish I went to Dale Adams the organiser and asked him to consider me for the Ultimate Combat II. He said he would. True to his word a few weeks later I had a fight contract through and I was in.

I decided to fight at Welterweight this time not Middle, so I was going to have to drop about 5kgs of body weight. I wanted to get some more speed and movement that I felt I lacked in previous fights. So started an eight-week intense programme of training to hit my target.

I started hard running, wind sprints and hill work to begin to burn the calories. Cycling and rowing were also thrown in for cardio and endurance. My good friend and sparring partner Rob Cannon for whom I owe so much trained with me constantly on upright and floor skills, conditioning and speed training.

We also went regularly to the Spanorium Home Farm near Bristol, which is run by Tex Woodward a top boxing coach and home to many great boxers over the years. We used the ring to work our mixed Martial

Arts skills and get a feel for it, this combined with my other training and a strict diet got m fighting fit to weigh in on the day at 74.9kgs. I felt as good as I ever did and regained a lot of speed and movement.

My opponent was a Commonwealth wrestler from Scotland Andy Proctor, a good lad and a seasoned fighter. My game plan was to try and stay on my feet and use my striking skills and if he 'shot' for my legs to sprawl and remain in the top position and keep punching. With Rob ringside guidance it all went to plan and I won the bout by unanimous decision. It was a great occasion to step into the ring at such a big event at forty-one years of age and receive the ovation I got from the crowd.

The support of my club members, friends and the Bristol crowd in general was phenomenal and I would like to thank you all in writing here and now, much appreciated.

The whole evening was a marvellous way to bring me up to my birthday. To have got a chance to fight in probably the world's toughest extreme sport was an honour and a pleasure. I took the fight for my own personal challenge and I was 100% up for it. I had peaked at the right time and I just wasn't going to lose this one. It was important for me and a test of my fitness, skill and dedication to MMA Combat. I must take this opportunity to thank organiser Dale Adams who put on a first class show. Dale is going to be the main man on the promoting front if he keeps up the good work. He already had a big hand in bring the Ultimate Fighting Championships to the Albert Hall, London this year and I'm sure he will go onto even bigger things.

You may ask why I would put myself through all that training at my time of life where many my age are content with a game of golf and a pint down the pub and talk about the 'good old days'. Well I suppose there's your answer. I want to feel alive and I still have the desire and passion to achieve. Life would be dull without a challenge and it makes the quieter moments sweeter. When you have spent the best part of your life involved in the Martial Arts and training for goals it is extremely hard to bring the curtain down or take a back seat. For me it is anyway. Where do I go form here? Well as the papers say 'Watch this space!'

Footnote

As I finish this book in Nov. 2002, I have been asked to judge a Cage Fight event in local Weston Super Mare. Two of my lads Matt and Steve will be appearing on this fight card. The promoter has just rung me again telling me a Welterweight fighter has just pulled out of a bout and they are looking for a last minute replacement. Did I know any decent 75kg fighters? Well let me think, 75kg, Welterweight mmmm, that's my weight, I suppose I could give it a bash…

Kevin O'Hagan. Nov 2002

'On the long journey from A to Z you learn an awful lot about B to Y'
(Quote by Geoff Thompson)

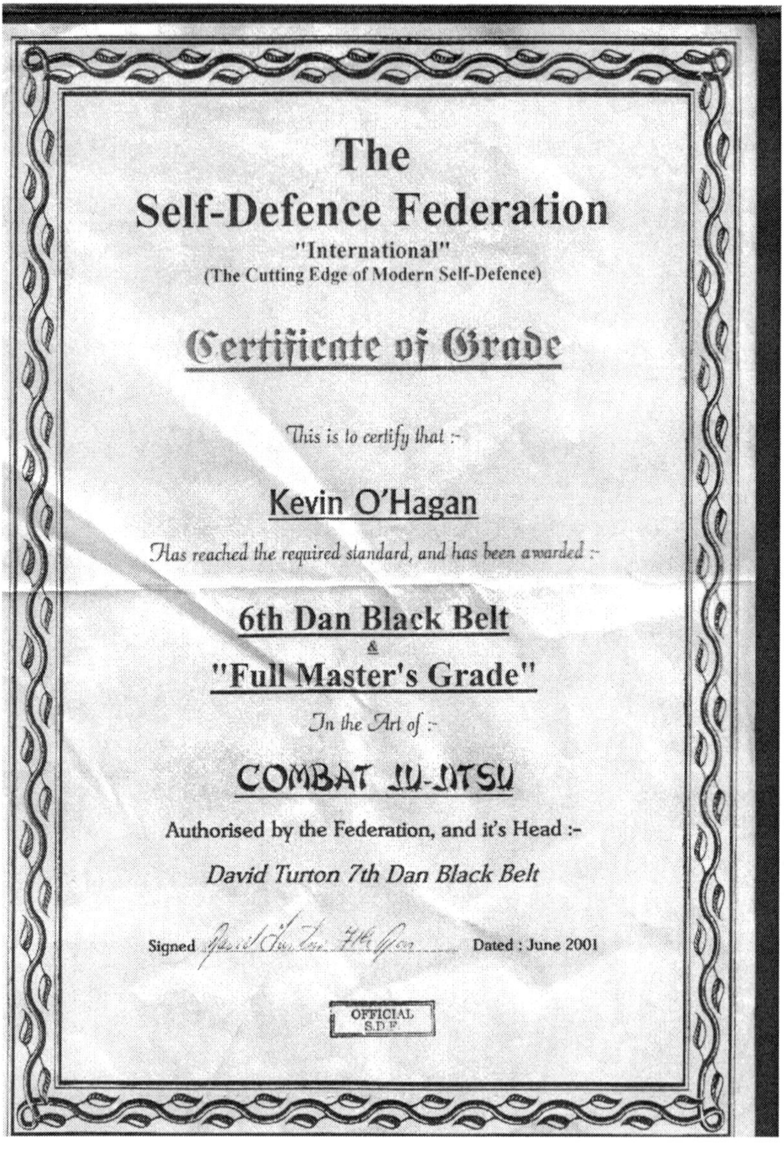

The
Self-Defence Federation
"International"
(The Cutting Edge of Modern Self-Defence)

Certificate of Grade

This is to certify that :-

Kevin O'Hagan

Has reached the required standard, and has been awarded :-

6th Dan Black Belt
&
"Full Master's Grade"

In the Art of :-

COMBAT JU-JITSU

Authorised by the Federation, and it's Head :-

David Turton 7th Dan Black Belt

Signed .... Dated : June 2001

OFFICIAL
S.D.F.

EXTREME DEFENCE

Tough measures for dangerous situations

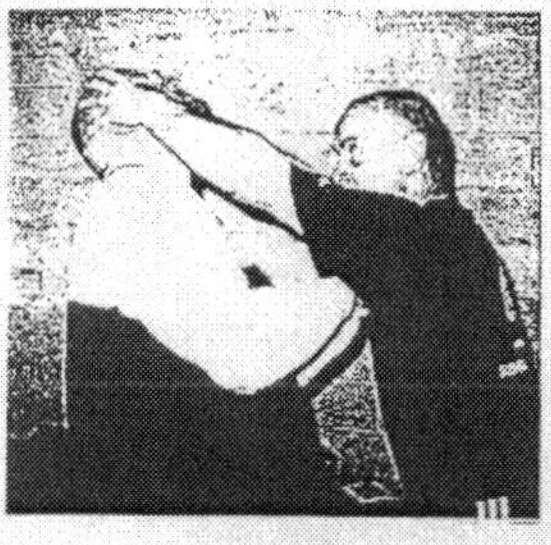

Welcome to the reality of street self defence with "Extreme Defence" This video tape gives you no-nonsense, no-holds barred responses against a multitude of dangerous and potentially life threatening situations. Witness fast, hard and rapid fire techniques as tough and uncompromising as the Pavement Arena itself. Learn revolutionary scenario based drills and training methods to improve and enhance your fighting skills for survival. Become your own Bodyguard!

This is the final word on effective and practical techniques in the ever increasing "Reality Revolution". If you are interested and serious about Street Self Defense and Close Quarter Combat that really works under extreme conditions, this tape is an absolute must!

Brought to you by Renowned Self Protection Instructor, Author and Submission Fighting competitor – Sensei Kevin O Hagan of The Bristol Goshin Jutsu Combat Academy

Warning

Due to the nature of some of this tape's content, it cannot be sold to persons under 18 years old.

For Details Phone : 0117 952 5711

Or E-mail : cannon@bristolcity24.freeserve.co.uk

SUDDEN IMPACT

No Holds Barred Fighting and Mixed Martial Arts Training

Brought to you by renowned Trainer, Fighter and Author

Kevin O Hagan

Following in the footsteps of his successful Impact Ju Jutsu tapes, comes his latest video "Sudden Impact" which puts together all of the ideas, drills and training methods from his previous "Impact Series" into a complete picture.
Watch Kevin and his guys working out at his famed "Impact Gym" in his NHB Classes. Witness hard conditioning, Vale Tudo focus mitt drills, stand up sparring, ground sparring and "All In" No Holds Barred sparring.
This video covers special drills for fight preparation and conditioning! Full clips of Live fights, tactics, tips and interviews are all included.

This tape is packed with proven and workable, reality based training for the Mixed Martial Arts Fighter, trainer or enthusiast. Every thing you see is real, live and spontaneous!

Price £15.00 inc P and P (UK)
£18.00 inc P and P (Overseas)

Send a cheque or Postal Order made Payable to Kevin O Hagan to:

23, Chester Road
St George
Bristol
BS5 7AX **For more details phone 0117 952 5711 or E-mail cannon@bristolcity24.freeserve.co.uk**

Deal with Conflict!

Today's society is one of increasing pressure, stress and aggression. Within your work, you may have to come into contact with angry, irate, aggressive or violent people. Do you have the vital training and knowledge necessary to deal with it? – No? Then don't delay! – Contact :

SAFE & SOUND MANAGEMENT UK

We are experts in personal or corporate training for:

- CONFLICT MANAGEMENT
- PERSONAL PROTECTION
- SAFETY AWARENESS
- CONFLICT RESOLUTION
- CONTROL AND RESTRAINT
- CLOSE QUARTER CONFRONTATION
- SPECIALIST SECURITY SKILLS

Get the right training for your staff, business, association, workplace, group or individual needs !

Safe & Sound Management UK is an organisation dedicated to conflict management. It's Chief Instructor Kevin O Hagan has over 20 years experience in Self Protection, Personal security and Close Quarter confrontation. He is a Senior Instructor with the renowned British Combat Association, the UK's premier organisation in this field. He is also an established author with four acclaimed books written on the subject.

Contact us on 0117 952 5711 or cannon@bristolcity24.freeserve.co.uk for seminars and training details.

The British Combat Association

This is to certify that

Kevin O'Hagan

is registered as

Senior Instructor

The British Combat Association are pleased to confirm that the above named person is registered as an 'Instructor' of the Association, having satisfied the Assessment Panel that his knowledge, skills and experience across a wide range of subjects, as determined by the Assessment Panel of the Association, is of a sufficiently high standard to merit inclusion onto the Register of Self Protection Instructors.
As a consequence, the Association would have no hesitation in recommending the above named person to teach and/or grade as the level of qualification allows in accordance with the rules and regulations set forth by the Association.

Assessment Panel

Certificate No. *0317/KO/SI*

Date: *June 2001*

Please note that Kevins Books and Videos Are available direct from Kevin O'Hagan

www.bristolgoshinjutsu.com

Email: cannon@bristolcity24.freeserve.co.uk

VIDEOS

1. OFFICAL GRADING SYLLABUS
2. IMPACT JU JUTSU VOL. I
   'Training and Conditioning for Combat'
3. IMPACT JU JUTSU VOL II
   'A full array of advanced exercises for combat conditioning'
4. IMPACT JU JUTSU VOL III
   'Innovative and Functional Training and Conditioning Methods'
5. DOWN AND OUT VOL. I
   'Standing to Floor Ju Jutsu Techniques'
6. DOWN AND OUT VOL. II
   'Advanced Standing to Floor Techniques'
7. FISTFUL OF DYNAMITE (YAWARA BO)
   'Dynamic techniques using this small but highly effective weapon'
8. WEAPON DISARMING
   'Brutal and effective techniques for disarming an array of modern and makeshift weaponry'
9. EXTREME DEFENCE Coming Soon!
   'Tough measures for dangerous situations.'

All Videos are instructed by SENSEI KEVIN O'HAGAN and are available at £14 each excluding P&P
(Add £1 per video for P&P in U.K. and £3 per video outside U.K.)

(Signed copies with personal message only available direct from Kevin O'Hagan)

Unsigned copies of books (not videos) can also be obtained from www.amazon.co.uk

**Gardners Bookshops
And
www.newbreedbooks.co.uk**

Other books from New Breed

PREVENT YOURSELF FROM BECOMING A VICTIM
'Dogs don't know Kung Fu'
A guide to Female Self Protection
By Jamie O'Keefe **£14** including post & packing

Never before has Female Self Protection used this innovative approach to pose questions like. Why do Rapist's Rape? Why are Women abused? Why do Stalkers Stalk? This book takes a look at all Simple, Serious, and Life threatening aspects of Self Protection that concern us daily, along with **PREVENTION** of Child abuse and Child Abduction, Emotional cruelty, Telephone abuse, Road rage, Muggers, Date rape, Weapon attacks, Female abduction, Sexual Assault & Rape, Self defence law, and what it will allow us to do to protect ourselves, plus much more. With over 46,500 words, 77 pictures and 200 printed pages 'Dog's Don't Know Kung fu' is a no nonsense approach to women's self defence. It covers many realistic scenarios involving Children's abduction as well as typical attacks on women. Besides quoting actual events, the book explains how to avoid trouble and how you should react if you get into a situation.

This book is a 'must read' for all women and parents.

It is also important for teenage women, but, due to some of its graphic depiction's of certain incidences, parents should read it first and decide if it's suitable for their child.

£14 from
NEW BREED

NO ONE FEARS WHEN ANGRY
by Jamie O'Keefe